MUSEUMS
IN
CRISIS

MUSEUMS IN CRISIS

EDITED, WITH AN INTRODUCTION, BY

Brian O'Doherty

FOREWORD BY

Nancy Hanks

George Braziller

NEW YORK

All rights reserved.
For information address the publisher:
George Braziller, Inc.
One Park Avenue
New York, N. Y. 10016

Standard Book Number: 0-8076-0629-4, cloth
0-8076-0628-6, paper
Library of Congress Catalog Card Number: 79-183186

First printing.
Printed in the United States of America.

The articles in this book first appeared in the Special Museum Issue of *Art in America,* vol. 59, no. 4 (July-August 1971). The editor wishes to thank the following members of the magazine's staff for their help with this issue: Francis Kloeppel, Executive Editor; Elton Robinson, Designer; Velma Stout, Production Editor; Carol N. Stallone, Assistant Editor; Nancy Foote, Assistant Editor; Carolyn Betsch, Researcher.

Contents

Foreword NANCY HANKS

Chairman, National Endowment for the Arts

The opportunity for demonstrating our responsibility for our cultural heritage and our cultural future has never been greater at any time in our history. Americans are participating to an unprecedented degree in cultural activities of all types. In efforts to meet increasing public demands and rising costs, our cultural institutions are being faced with questions and problems that have never existed before, or, more accurately, have never existed in such dimension.

Museums share a common challenge with orchestras, theaters, opera, and dance companies. In a time of increasing financial difficulty, museums are attempting to fulfill multiple responsibilities—to the public, to their collections, to their staffs, to artists, scientists, and historians, and to the past, as well as the present and future. As the task of establishing priorities becomes more intricate and involved, it becomes increasingly important to ask the right questions. Or else we run the risk of upsetting the balance of museum activities and goals.

The National Endowment for the Arts, a federal agency, and its advisory body, the National Council on the Arts, view the situation with a sense of considerable urgency. Other agencies of the federal government do so as well.

The Arts Endowment considers the preservation and advancement of our cultural heritage as its major responsibility. With the sympathetic consideration and support of the President and the Congress, funds available to the Endowment increased sufficiently so that a pilot program for art, history, and science museums could be initiated in 1971, under the guidance of a practicing museum director.

The Museum Program, conceived in close cooperation with museum professionals, is viewed as a flexible instrument capable of responding inventively to current needs and of recognizing new needs as they appear. The National Council on the Arts, with the advice and concurrence of the Museum Panel, identified areas of particular concern and established a number of categories of assistance to respond to needs, however modestly. In this way, a blueprint for the future is being developed by the museum community for the museums, since, in effect, the museum profession determines its own priorities and assists in developing and administering the federal program.

In 1971, the Arts Endowment distributed nearly a million dollars through its pilot Museum Program; this figure will more than triple in 1972. Though the funds are small in relation to the need, they help focus national attention on the museum community; they stimulate increased private and other public support; they provide information on museums' needs, assembling facts and figures necessary to plan effectively.

Programs are now in operation to encourage the purchase of contemporary art; to support training; to aid special exhibitions; to assist important conservation efforts; to allow specialists of all kinds to assist museums for extended periods; and to further museums' growing public-service and community activities. A small fellowship program is planned and consideration is being given to establishing ways in which modes of permanent installation and display can be helped by the Endowment.

The situation of our museums, some threatened with permanent closure and others curtailing their activities and availability to the public, is evidence of a serious but characteristic dilemma: the greater the public interest, the greater the financial burden. Nor is there an easy or even rapid solution in sight. Since this book presents a dialogue on these problems from all concerned—museum professionals, critics, scholars, artists, trustees, and others—it is a welcome occasion. Only through such dialogue can the flow of ideas be encouraged and criticism of all kinds evaluated. In other words, our problems must be defined before we can solve them.

Introduction BRIAN O'DOHERTY

The Museum age, which reached its Augustan apogee with the post-World War II boom in art education, in special exhibitions, in collecting, in museum-building, is finally over. Museums, once permanent fixtures by which to negotiate our spiritual journeys, have suddenly revealed infirmities in their foundations that have threatened them with collapse. Like many institutions in the late sixties, they were abruptly thrust from their historical context into the vicissitudes of contemporary life, where the problems of the entire society—many of them irrelevant to art museums—were brought to bear on them.

This exposure has provoked a self-examination that may prove profitable. But museums, deprived of the confidence in their history that guides institutions as they move into the future, are having difficulty in taking bearings on their present condition. There are many reasons for this. Museums have been forced to cope with a variety of political problems for which their staffs are hardly qualified. Museum men also appear uncertain of their responsibilities to their own holdings. By and large administered by antiquated methods, their policies guided by trustees who have not demonstrated their capacity to understand contemporary issues, most museums have had their position defined for them.

Added to all this is the most severe financial embarrassment that museums have ever suffered. (Diminishing endowments and private funds, increasing operating costs and public services have forced many museums to seek corporate support. The acquisition of state monies apart from the New York State Council's pioneering gesture last year, remains the most important gap in building a broad base for museum support, now that city funds are, for the first time, being augmented by Federal aid, which should increase.) It is hard to avoid the conclusion that the museum is in a state of physical, financial, esthetic and spiritual disarray. Its survival as a viable institution, maintaining standards of scholarship and high public service, is in doubt, and it is but a short step to salutary meditations on the fate of culture in our society.

Museums, in their postwar expansionist phase, were

led into the position of having to promise more than they could provide—esthetically and culturally as well as physically. Now their financial and philosophical difficulties are forcing a drastic rethinking of their priorities. In assessing these, some urgent matters, masked by the optimism of the preceding decades, are demanding attention. While no national survey of conservation needs exists, large monies are needed to maintain and repair the works requiring attention. In addition to this, the museums can no longer compete for the best talents, many of which now go to the universities; the profession is underpaid, overworked and beleaguered from within and without. Under present circumstances, it is not likely to be prolific in ideas on how to cope with the current, prolonged emergency.

These matters, however, are secondary to the fundamental issue: What should a museum's functions be? When funds are plentiful, high levels of scholarship and of education hardly come into conflict. When they are not, the museum's traditional conflict between scholarship/ conservation and education becomes exacerbated. Many feel there has been an erosion of scholarly responsibilities, and a capitulation to the demands of education, or what its critics would call entertainment.

Some museum professionals are of the opinion that more limited goals and a rethinking of the way in which museums offer art to the public are necessary, indeed imperative. In part this is based on the realization that art—anywhere—is vulnerable to its context. A Rembrandt in a White Tower diner can hardly reveal its values or lend its civilities to the environment. While museums once erred in imposing their temple atmosphere on works of art, things have now gone the other way. One of the most valuable and irreplaceable contexts for art is the integrity and sympathy of fine scholarship. The careful placing of works of art in fresh contexts (including special exhibitions where both study and the public are well served) is a vital part of that constant sifting and reevaluation of art that preserves the heritage in the best sense—by putting it to judicious use and mobilizing it through fresh and inventive examination. A major priority is to restore and augment

Museums and radicals: A history of emergencies

LINDA NOCHLIN

"Often founded on rationalized pillage,
Augustan pride and democratic pieties, the
art museum, erected at the crossroads
of numerous contradictions, has always been
subject to abrupt and radical revisions."

The myth of art history came into being at the same time as its temple, the museum.[1] Both were conceived in the optimistic days of the Enlightenment and borne to shore by the waves of the French Revolution. The first great art museum for the general public—the Louvre—was the creation of the first great radical upheaval of our time.[2] In a sense, the creation of the museum was a token of art's impotence, its final severance from the social structure, setting it apart, like religion, for weekend worship. Yet, in another sense, the museum was from the start conceived of as an instrument of cultural reintegration on a higher level, a means of spreading historical and esthetic knowledge among an ever-broadening segment of society, allowing to all a share of the cultural manna which had formerly been the food of a privileged few.[3] As the shrine of an elitist religion and at the same time a utilitarian instrument for democratic education, the museum may be said to have suffered from schizophrenia from the start.

The relation of art vis-à-vis radicalism has always been complex and shifting; consequently, the museum has always occupied an ambiguous position in radical thought and action. Today, for example, much depends on whether one is looking at the museum from the viewpoint of the radical (or advanced) artist, from that of the radical member of the public, or that of the radical museum worker. The radical artist may, for example, want to do away with the whole concept of the museum (which he conceives of as a mortuary for dead cultural artifacts) and the whole notion of art-as-objects, calling for a merging of life and art, or the death of art. The political radical, on the contrary, may call for an art of greater social relevance and immediate comprehensibility and may sneer at non-art, anti-art, environments, concepts, software and process as simply more of the same bourgeois elitism and mystification. The socially committed museum worker may feel that his project lies in the realm of popularization and dissemination—i.e., of bringing both traditional and avantgarde works into the life of groups hitherto deprived of meaningful contact with them—and may wish to include an ever-widening range of objects and activities within the scope of museum functions. While some of these goals may sometimes overlap, they are more often contradictory—indeed, mutually exclusive. Yet one may say that such contradictions, or others like them, were inherent in museums even during the palmy days of their creation and expansion in the nineteenth century.

While the creators of the Louvre at the end of the eighteenth century were hardly bothered by many of the questions that plague museum directors today, the founding of that institution was fraught with squabbling and controversy, which caused considerable delay in carrying out the enterprise. Significantly enough, the day chosen for the opening, August 10, 1793, was the anniversary of the fall of the monarchy: on this day the former palace of the kings, now transformed into the "Museum National: Monument Consacré à l'Amour et à l'Etude des Arts," was opened to the public.[4] The source of the art works of the original Louvre was, of course, equally significant as far as political implications were concerned: about three-quarters of the paintings shown came from the Royal collection, while the remainder came from the suppressed churches, with a certain scattering of works from the collection of the suppressed Academy of Painting and the pictures abandoned by émigrés.[5] Thus the first great public museum was created through the transfer of cultural property from the hands of the ruling aristocracy into those of the people, or at least their representatives.

At this time, certain crucial ethical-esthetic issues were raised, issues which have remained to haunt museums ever since. In the first place, there was the question of where the art was to come from. Certainly no right-thinking radical, or even mild liberal, could object to the transformation of privileged splendor into public educational material. As a later English historian of the Louvre remarked, "All the kings regarded the accumulated productions of the human mind they possessed simply as the flattering proof of their riches and power. Caprice and disorder, infatuation and disgust, avarice and prodigality, compromised every day the safety of the inappreciable deposit which unlimited wealth placed in their hands.''[6] Masterpieces were entitled to public honor and professional protection. But while the liberation of art works for the edification of the people was to become a more burning issue with the Napoleonic art confiscations, it arose already in the case of Alexandre Lenoir's Musée des Monumens Français, which opened in the former monastery of the Petits Augustins in 1795.[7] While Lenoir was a fanatic believer in the public utilization of his museum—a collection begun in 1790 from the confiscated art properties of the Church, with the object of preserving the fragments of vandalized Royal and ecclesiastic monuments from further damage, as well as to provide instruction by exposing the public to hitherto unappreciated treasures of French medieval art—his enemies, most notably Quatremère de Quincy, pressed forward the doctrine of the work of art as inseparable from its milieu, with the implication that Lenoir had in fact destroyed organic (if crumbling) totalities in order to create a museum of dismembered fragments. The implications of this controversy pursued the museum-makers of the nineteenth and twentieth century: accusations of vandalism, looting, cultural imperialism, destruction of meaning, and outright theft echo down the corridors of our greatest institutions, and are implicit in the very nature of the museum and, indeed, its democratizing enterprise. For if works of art are to be gathered together for the moral, cultural and esthetic benefit of the people of Paris or London or New York, then they must, of necessity, be ripped loose from their original functions or settings or be taken away from some previous owner—either willing or not.

Nationalism and patriotism made their appearance early in the apparently esthetic ambience of the museum. The vast expansion of the Louvre—retitled the Musée Napoléon—under Napoleon's quite systematic program of art confiscations reveals the moral tensions implicit in the notion of the broader dissemination of art, within a fiercely nationalistic framework. There is no question about the fact that it was Napoleon, who under the pretext of various treaties and armistice agreements, succeeded in despoiling much of Europe of its prime art treasures.[8] Yet the systematic confiscation of works of art began in the Revolutionary "campaigns of liberation," most notably the one in Belgium in 1794, at which point a program of "expert official looting," to use the words of Cecil Gould, was undertaken.[9] While the words of the revolutionary artist Luc Barbier, who was intimately involved in the theft of art treasures from Belgium, before the Convention in 1794, may strike us as clichéd at best and hypocritical at worst, there is a striking familiarity in the tenor of his remarks. Barbier refers to the confiscated paintings as "immortal works left us by the brush of Rubens, Van Dyck and other founders of the Flemish school," and notes that "these masterpieces have been sullied overlong by the aspect of servitude: it is in the bosom of free folk that the works of celebrated men should remain; the tears of slaves are unworthy of their glory."[10] "Letters and the arts are the friends of Liberty," declared the Committee of Public Instruction, on 9 Messidor, Year II. "The monuments addressed to them by slaves will acquire in our midst a glory which a despotic government could not bestow upon them."[11] Indeed, the principal targets of the commissaires in Italy, as Gould points out, were precisely the Hellenistic and Roman sculpture—concrete tokens of the "republican" virtues of antiquity— in which "the Frenchman of the Revolution saw his spiritual ancestors."[12]

In the course of this vast "liberation" of art property, an unavoidable relationship was created between revolutionary values and vandalism. On a somewhat different level, the Revolutionary and Napoleonic plunderers could justify themselves by maintaining that they were taking over works for the higher cause of art itself, on the ground that the original possessors had neglected or mistreated their treasures.[13] "It is most fortunate for the cause of Art," declares a catalogue statement from the Louvre, referring to some of the Lombard works captured in 1798, "that these masterpieces are being removed from a country where they were totally neglected and it only requires the practised hand of our craftsmen to restore them to the true lovers of the arts.''[14] Yet, while much of this sounds like, and in fact is, rationalization for blatant pillaging, at the same time it is true that the Musée Napoléon in its heyday enabled Frenchmen, and others as well, artists and ordinary citizens, to see assembled in one spot art works which they would have had to travel considerable distances to reach, or to which access might have been completely barred, when the works were the possessions of private owners, prelates or nobles, who simply saw them as their personal possessions rather than as part of the universal heritage of mankind.

In 1815, at the time when the works in the Musée Napoléon were being restored to their original owners, a Scottish miniature painter at the Louvre reports meeting Sir Thomas Lawrence—hardly a French patriot—''who said that every artist must lament the breaking up of a collection in a place so central for Europe, for everything was laid open to the public with a degree of liberality unknown elsewhere . . .''[15] Certainly the Parisian populace took pride in their artistic trophies of war. The triumphal entry of the confiscated art works had been celebrated in a remarkable ceremony in the Year VI of the Republic. Enormous chariots bearing paintings still in their packing cases, but carefully

Triumphal entry in Paris of art seized by Napoleon; contemporary engraving. "Enormous chariots bearing paintings still in their packing cases, but carefully labeled in large letters . . . received wild applause from an enormous crowd, with even greater enthusiasm reserved for the massive carts bearing such statues as the Apollo Belvedere and the Laocoön, decked out with laurel wreaths, flowers and flags."

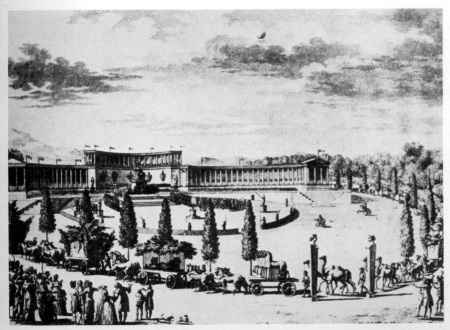

labeled in large letters "Transfiguration of Raphael" or "Christ by Titian," received wild applause from an enormous crowd, with even greater enthusiasm reserved for the massive carts bearing such statues as the Apollo Belvedere and the Laocoön, decked out with laurel wreaths, flowers and flags.[16] This same proletarian mob stood outside the Louvre in 1815, watching their treasures being carried off to their previous owners with "fury and despair in their looks, like the brewing of an insurrection," according to an eye-witness.[17]

Yet the people were not always so solicitous about the possession and the well-being of works of art in periods of revolutionary agitation, again demonstrating the ambiguous status of the museum vis-à-vis radical ideology and action. Protection of the national art heritage, with the understood promise of an extension of the privileges of culture (rather than iconoclasm, an association of the museum with the overthrown elite), has always been the project of revolutionary governments. Saving art—or the museum—from vandalism, the vandalism of the mob in whose name and with whose blood the various revolutions were fought, was the first step in the duties of the directors of committees appointed by the radical insurgents both in 1848, under the Provisional Government, and in 1871, under the Commune.

No less a democrat than Harriet Beecher Stowe, in her little-known travel memoirs of her trip to Europe in the middle of the century, summarized the right-thinking liberal position about the Louvre and the 1848 Revolution, both of which she admired, in the following terms in 1853:

During the heat of the outburst that expelled Louis Philippe from the throne, the Louvre was in some danger of destruction. Destructiveness is a native element of human nature, however repressed by society; and hence every great revolutionary movement always brings to the surface some who are for indiscriminate demolition. Moreover there is a strong tendency in the popular mind, where art and beauty have for many years been monopolized as the prerogative of a haughty aristocracy, to identify art and beauty with oppression . . . So in the first burst of popular enthusiasm that expelled the monarchy, the cry was raised by some among the people, "We shall never get rid of kings until we pull down the palaces" . . . The populace rushed into the splendid halls and saloons of the Louvre, and a general encampment was made among the pictures. In this crisis a republican artist named Jeanron saved the Louvre; saved the people the regret that must have come over them had they perpetrated barbarisms, and Liberty the shame of having such outrages wrought in her name. Appointed by the provisional government to the oversight of the Louvre, and well known among the people as a republican, he boldly came to the rescue. "Am I not one of you?" he said. "Am I not one of the people? Are they not the pride and glory of our country? Shall we destroy our most glorious possession in the first hour of its passing into our hands?"

After approving the important repairs and improvements Jeanron had made in the great museum, Mrs. Stowe continues:

These facts have been communicated to me from a perfectly reliable source. As an American, and a republican, I cannot but take pleasure in them. I mention them because it is often supposed, from the destructive effects which attend the first advent of democratic principles where they have to explode their way into existence through masses

Ruins of the Tuileries after 1871; photo, Musée Carnavalet, Paris. ". . . the cry was raised by some among the people, 'We shall never get rid of kings until we pull down the palaces' . . ."

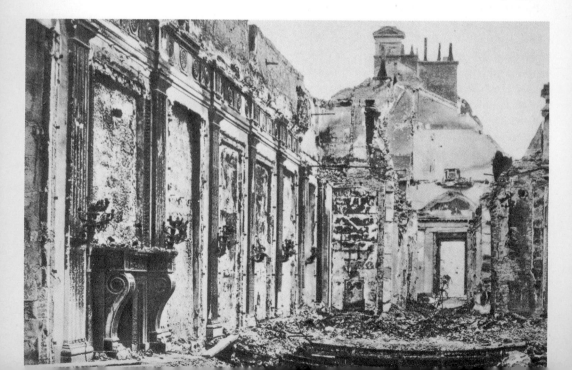

of ancient rubbish, that popular liberty is unfavorable to art. It could never be so in France, because the whole body of the people are the most thoroughly artistic in their tastes and feelings than in most countries. They are almost slaves to the outwardly beautiful, taken captive by the eye and the ear, and only the long association of beauty with tyranny, with suffering, want, and degradation to themselves, could ever have inspired any of them with even a momentary bitterness against it.[18]

However momentary, the first "advent of democratic principles" during the Revolution of the eighteenth century had indeed led to large-scale destruction of both religious and secular monuments and works of art,[19] and the National Assembly, once it had decreed the nationalization of the property of the clergy, almost at once had to make provisions for the preservation and protection of the works of art which fell under this heading.[20] It was precisely in these emergency circumstances that the Commission des Monuments came into being. Rescued from the fury of the people by revolutionary art lovers and scholars, the visual objectifications of tyranny, superstition and oppression were, through the alchemy of the museum, transformed into the National Heritage, the most precious possession of the people.[21]

By the time of the 1848 Revolution, the notion that the museums were the possession of the people was a clearly established idea. One of the first actions of the Provisional Government was to remove the administration of the museums from the *liste civile,* that is, the King's privy purse, and place them under the jurisdiction of the Minister of the Interior. The whole art administration was restructured along more democratic, practical and forward-looking lines. As early as March 24 the revolutionary government, in recognition of the fact that "it is important to concentrate in a single, vast place all the products of thought which are the splendors of a great people," decreed that "the Palace of the Louvre would be completed," that it would take the name of the "Palais du Peuple," that it would be used for the exhibition of painting, or products of industry and for the national library. In addition, an appeal was made to the workers to come and take part in the task of completing the Louvre.[22]

The program undertaken by the painter Philippe
Auguste Jeanron, who was appointed general director of the national museums and of the Louvre by the
revolutionaries, was an impressive one, and not only in
the eyes of Mrs. Stowe. Jeanron himself was a known
radical, and a painter of scenes from the life of the proletariat.[23] Indeed, it was under his brief directorate that
previously ignored painters like the "peasant artists"
the Le Nains were given a chance to be seen and admired.[24] Jeanron had taken part in the July Revolution
of 1830, and soon afterward became the head of the
radical Société Libre de Peinture et de Sculpture. He
played a truly heroic and active role in protecting art
treasures from violence during the 1848 uprising. When
undisciplined bands, bivouacked in the Great Gallery,
attempted to set fire to the building, he argued with the
invaders so convincingly that they extinguished their
torches and retired; later he merely had to write on the
walls "Respect aux arts!" to be understood by all.

Yet Jeanron was far more than a heroic defender of
art property, and more than the inspired administrator
his reorganizational program reveals. He was a firm
believer in the role of the museum as a democratic
instrument. For him, the idea that the treasures of the
Louvre belonged to all the people was no mere matter
of rhetoric: it was the guiding principle of his organization. For example, he cleared out the private people who
still made their home in the Louvre and had their studios
there—a practice which he felt was not only unfair, but
prejudicial to the interests of the entire body of artists
and art lovers, since these facilities could be used for
public purposes. Jeanron's admirable balance between
regard for the internal welfare of the museum and its
duty toward the public is well illustrated by his attitude
toward a proposal to collect all the drawings of the
Louvre into three hundred volumes. It was argued that
these works should be shown to a few eminent and
favored persons, and that the common herd of artists
and art lovers should be systematically kept away from
them. An Academician maintained that the public already had too much to see: "Keep these precious documents for people like ourselves who alone are capable

of appreciating them."[25] Jeanron was strongly against this proposal, on democratic grounds, maintaining that "all the national treasures should be accessible to the just curiosity of the people, to the study of the workers; and this manner of collecting together objects of that nature [i.e., putting drawings into volumes] is in opposition to every serious communication with the public which is interested in seeing them."[26] In principle, Jeanron felt that whatever the museum could not communicate to the public because of lack of exhibition space or reasons of like nature should not even be kept by the museum. The same desire for ease of communication is evident in his projected change in the manner of displaying paintings in the galleries, where he hoped to replace confusion with order, clarity and ease of access, or in his attempt to inventory and identify the vast clutter of objects in the museum's possession, or to create a meaningful catalogue, and to do the same for the provincial museums as well as for those of the capital. What Jeanron might have accomplished we will never know: he was removed from his position after the fall of the Revolutionary Government, suspected of giving refuge to its head, Ledru-Rollin.

When the radical Commune briefly took over Paris in 1871, once more the first action with regard to the museums was the double one of protection and democratization—a more far-reaching but also more utopian and ephemeral project than that undertaken by the revolutionaries of 1848. Significantly enough, it was Gustave Courbet, that arch-radical and rejector of the past who had openly jeered at Raphael and Michelangelo, who worked day and night to protect the museum treasures from destruction during this period of unrest and uprising. Courbet had been elected Chairman of the Art Commission and charged with the protection of the works of art in Paris after the surrender of Napleon III; with the assistance of fellow artists of the commission, he worked hard to remove works from museums in and near Paris and store them in the Louvre, took steps to guard against fire and theft, packed up valuable objects, and placed sandbags against

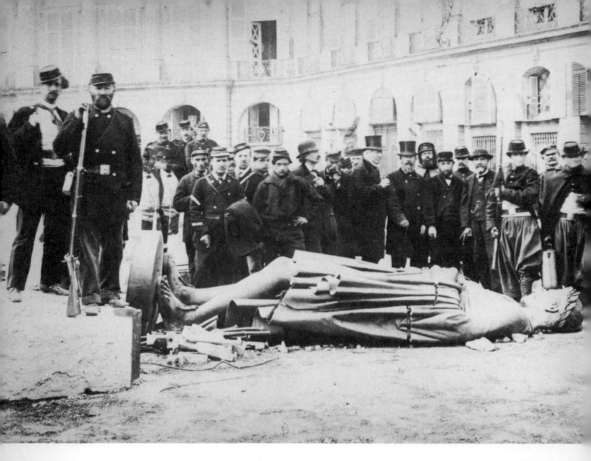

those which could not be moved.[27] When the Commune took over in Paris, Courbet, who had been elected a delegate, in effect became the head of art activities under the radical government. One of the first steps he took was to call a meeting of the artists, inviting them to "take over themselves the direction of museums and the collections of art, which, while being the property of the nation, are theirs above all, from the double point of view of intellectual and material life."[28] At the same time Courbet suggested that an elected assembly of artists "might name the directors and curators of museums, suppress the Ecole de Rome and the Ecole des Beaux Arts, and abolish all decorations and medals for artists."[29] At a far larger meeting about a week later, a large group under the aegis of Courbet formed themselves into the Fédération des Artistes de Paris and issued

*Destruction of the Vendôme
Column with statue of
Napoleon by the Communards,
1871; photo, Gernsheim
Collection, University of
Texas, Austin. Courbet
is the bearded man in the
second row. "Whatever
Courbet's role in the
destruction of the Vendôme
Column—hardly a work of
art, in any case—and no
matter how ambivalent
his own attitude toward
the art of tradition
may have been, he was
obviously sincere
and scrupulous about
preserving and protecting
the art treasures for which
he was responsible under
trying circumstances."*

a manifesto in which they declared that the government of the art world by artists had the triple mission of conservation of the treasures of the past, the ordering and revelation of all the elements of the present, and the regeneration of the future through teaching. New, more democratic museum personnel were to be appointed, the museums revised and rearranged for the benefit of the public; large lecture halls were to be constructed for higher education in art, and a new art journal, the *Officiel des Arts,* "progressive, independent, worthy and sincere," would aid in the general artistic mission of information and education. The manifesto ended with plans for the universal dissemination of art:

Finally, through speech, writing, and illustration, by means of the popular reproduction of masterpieces, through intellectually and morally uplifting images to be

the present, and which could only be overcome by the radical gesture of burning it to the ground."[35] Marinetti's welcome to "the kindly incendiarists with the carbon fingers"[36] had been anticipated over a half a century earlier by the Realist critic and spokesman Duranty, who in his "Notes sur l'Art," printed in the short-lived journal *Réalisme* in 1856, declared: "I have just come from the Louvre . . . If I had had some matches, I would have set fire to that catacomb, with the intimate conviction that I was serving the cause of the art of the future." And Pissarro, a radical in politics throughout his life, although often enthusiastic about older art, reportedly maintained that "we must bring down the necropolises of art."[37]

Yet it was Monet, hardly a political agitator though a steadfast republican, who made the most significant gesture vis-à-vis the Louvre and all that it stood for: in 1866–67, he paid several visits to that museum—not to look at the works of art, but rather to look out of the window.[38] Deliberately turning his back upon the treasures of the past in their indoor setting, Monet painted three extraordinary cityscapes of modern Paris from the east balcony of the Louvre, plein-air records of the contemporary city; in their aggressive randomness, visual accuracy and lack of incident or traditional pictorial structure, they asserted a potent visual challenge to that musty museum and all the values it stood for. Monet's gesture was as momentously symbolic in its way, though less mythic, as that of Petrarch closing his volume of St. Augustine's *Confessions* to look out at the splendid panorama of nature from the top of Mount Ventoux. From that time on, despite Manet's constant reference to the art of the masters of the past or Renoir's declaration that one learns to paint in museums rather than before nature or Cézanne's numerous copies from the art of tradition, the relation of avant-garde artists toward their cultural heritage, and hence toward the museums as repositories of a viable and transmittable living tradition, becomes a problematic one.

Not until the twentieth century did anti-museum feeling on the part of radical artists become solidified into a politico-esthetic program in the doctrine of the Italian

Futurists and the Russian Revolutionaries: "We will destroy museums, libraries . . ." proclaimed Marinetti in the Futurist Manifesto of 1908.[39] We will free Italy from her numberless museums which cover her with countless cemeteries . . . Museums, cemeteries!" he continues. "Identical truly, in the sinister promiscuousness of so many objects unknown to each other."[40]

Despite the violence of his anti-museum, anti-cultural rhetoric, Marinetti and the Futurists, like Signac, Steinlen and the French anarchist artists before them, were still thinking of art in the traditional sense, that is to say, as created objects of painting and sculpture, no matter how they might think of altering its style, content or ideological implications.[41] It is from England, and from the writings of that radical activist and anti-High Art father of them all, William Morris, that the winds of basic cultural change blow. Significantly enough, it was also in England that the first major breakthrough in the concept of the museum itself had occurred, with the creation of the Victoria and Albert, founded in a spirit of liberalism, and attempting to bridge the gap between the fine and the applied arts, between taste and industry, between the workman and the quality of his workmanship. As early as 1835—a date not unconnected with that charter of the newly powerful middle class, the Reform Bill of 1832—a Select Committee on Arts and Manufactures had been appointed by Parliament in order "to enquire into the best means of extending a knowledge of the arts, and of the principles of design among the people (especially the manufacturing population of the country)";[42] and in 1852, a Museum of Manufactures, later changed in title to the Museum of Ornamental Art, was created "for the selection, description, and preservation for their own sake of the finest products of artistic craftsmanship."[43] It was, of course, no accident that a museum designed for the purpose of improving the taste of manufacturers, artisans and the public should first have appeared in England, the most advanced industrial nation of the world. Indeed, a practical, businesslike approach to the grandeur of art was exhibited from the start by the Select Committee in its report of 1836: "To us, a peculiarly manufacturing nation, the connexion between art and manufactures is most important;—and for this merely economical reason (were there no higher motive), it equally imports us to encourage art in its loftier attributes . . ."[44] The Victoria and Albert doubtless took its task of popular dissemination seriously—a branch of the South Kensington Museum was actually set up in the East End of London at Bethnal Green in 1872, so that the mass of laborers and artisans could take advantage of its exhibitions. When Charles P. Taft lectured on the subject of art museums in a democracy in Cincinnati in 1878, he chose the Victoria and Albert as his model, pointing out that the general conception of a museum at this time was "a series of rooms, filled with costly paintings of the old masters," but that the South Kensington Museum (as the Victoria and Albert was then called) was a museum of a different character: "It represents to the artisan or handicraftsman perfection in all the known branches of industry."[45]

Yet for William Morris—though he was doubtless not untouched by the ferment of contemporary interest in the decorative arts—the whole notion of a museum, insofar as it emphasized the unhealthy separation between art and life, thinking and doing, feeling and making, was a questionable one, compounding the general spiritual, social and esthetic malaise of the capitalist industrial societies of his day. Still, the museum might act as an irritant, a goad to action, by moving the citizen of contemporary London "to discontent of what is careless and brutal now"; and Morris admits that his city is at least well off for museums, although he complains that they are not open "on the only day on which an ordinarily busy man, one of the taxpayers who support them," can see them. Yet he also complains that there are inherent difficulties in museums as spreaders of esthetic enlightenment: "It is true . . . that people need some preliminary instruction before they can get all the good possible to be got from the prodigious treasures of art possessed by the country in that form: there also one sees things in a piecemeal way: nor can I deny that there is something melancholy about a museum, such a tale of violence, destruction, and carelessness, as its treasured scraps tell us.''[46] There is something aside from the point about the museum notion of art, about art separated from any sense of the larger responsibility to the quality of life in all aspects and for all people:

Unless something or other is done to give all men some pleasure for the eyes and rest for the mind in the aspect of their own and their neighbor's houses, until the contrast is less disgraceful between the fields where beasts live and the streets where men live, I suppose that the practice of the arts must be mainly kept in the hands of a few highly cultivated men, who can go often to beautiful places, whose education enables them, in the contemplation of the past glories of the world, to shut out from their view the everyday squalors that the most of men move in.

he states in a lecture, ''The Lesser Arts,'' in 1878. Yet he himself believes that art

sickens under selfishness and luxury, that she will not live thus isolated and exclusive. I will go further than this and say that on such terms I do not wish her to live. I protest that it would be a shame for an honest artist to enjoy what he had huddled up to himself of such art, as it would be for a rich man to sit and eat dainty food among starving soldiers in a beleaguered fort.[47]

Only in a world organized on principles of liberty, equality and fraternity will men achieve the necessary condition for the creation of true art, Morris maintains; this condition is happiness in work, which ''will assuredly bring forth decorative, noble, *popular* art.''[48]

In Morris' utopian England of the future, so movingly brought to life in *News from Nowhere*, where every man and every woman is a creative craftsman, where dress, housing and furniture are simple, functional and esthetically satisfying, where love between the sexes is free and money no longer exists—in a true socialist society, where each receives, and gives, joyfully according to his needs and desires—high art (the need for art and the adulation of it as a thing apart from daily experience) has simply withered away, and museums, like prisons or schools, have disappeared. ''Ah,'' says one of the fortunate inhabitants of this utopian England of the future, upon being asked by the narrator about a certain stately building he encounters, "that is an old building built before the middle of the twentieth century, and as you see, in a queer fantastic style not over beautiful, but there are some fine things inside it, too, mostly pictures, some very old. It is called the National Gallery; I have sometimes puzzled as to what the name means: anyhow, nowadays whenever there is a place where pictures are kept as curiosities permanently it is called a National Gallery, perhaps after this one . . ."[49] What used to be called art has no name among the citizens of Morris' utopia, for it had "become a necessary part of the labour of every man who produces."[50] For Morris, it was clear that such a non-restrictive, non-museum-bound concept of art could come into being only under the reign of socialism and after the destruction of the profit motive.

Indeed, it was not until the establishment of the first socialist regime, the Soviet Union, that Morris' general ideas (if not his handicraft emphasis and nostalgic harking back to the spirit of the Middle Ages) were put into effect. Despite insistence upon the primary role of the machine, on the propagandistic mission of the arts and a proclivity for violence and abstraction, the art doctrines of the Soviet avant-garde echo Morris' democratic, anti-elitist, and life-relating tendencies: "In the new order of society, in which work will cease to be slavery, in which there will no longer be small groups producing luxuries for a restricted stratum of society, but where work is being done *by everyone for everyone,* in such a society work is given free scope and everything which is produced is art," proclaimed El Lissitzky.[51] The Russian avant-garde of the early twenties certainly carried out and further developed Morris' vision in Constructivism, defined by the poet Mayakovsky as "the formal work of the artist as an artisan which serves to mould our practical lives."[52] Like Morris, the Constructivists opposed the European notion of the fine arts. In Lissitzky's words: "The European thesis was 'Fine Art for Ever.' The arts were made into a quite private, subjective-esthetic affair.

Our antithesis was 'Up with Everything Except Fine Art.' "[53] In the manifesto of the Fex group, "yesterday" was exemplified by museums, temples and libraries, as opposed to "today": factories, plants, yards.[54] The great theatrical producer V. V. Meyerhold maintained that the "proletariat must completely fill the ditch that an outworn class has dug between art and life."[55] Yet at the same time that the art revolutionaries were enlivening the streets of the cities with dynamic propaganda posters and paint buckets, that vast Mass Spectacles were taking place, that Tatlin's Constructivist Monument was rising, Malevich drew up a program for Mass Education in art which included the foundation of art museums throughout the country, touring exhibits for the showing of the latest products of the new art and, in Moscow, the foundation of a Central Museum for the cultivation of painting.[56] Obviously, the museum was still not a dead issue.

The notion of the museum dies hard, in even the most revolutionary societies, and the reason for this is not hard to understand: it is once more the idea that the people—all the people—have the right to be granted access—and not merely physical but spiritual access—to objects possessed of value in their own right which the masses have hitherto been prevented from enjoying. While it may be true that the Cuban Revolution brought art out of the museums, released it from the limitations of easel painting, and integrated it into the Cuban social system in the form of political propaganda paintings on the walls of apartment houses, which spoke "the same language as Fidel Castro or the sugar-cane cutter,"[57] and even if the flourishing poster art of Cuba achieves a satisfactory compromise between the demands of art and life, providing the urban landscape with a vital form of public imagery which manages to combine avant-garde esthetic self-sufficiency with revolutionary fervor,[58] still the same revolutionary society saw fit to create an Art Education Room in the National Museum of Cuba in order to make access to museum art a real possibility for all the people.[59] This room, divided into four extremely carefully thought-out sections, explains the various types of museums; the dif-

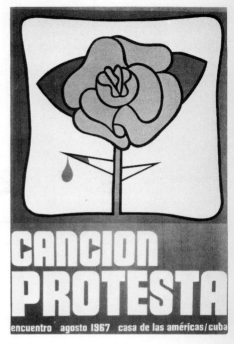

Song of Protest, *Cuban poster.*
". . . the flourishing poster art of Cuba achieves a satisfactory compromise between the demands of art and life, providing the urban landscape with a vital form of public imagery which manages to combine avant-garde esthetic self-sufficiency with revolutionary fervor . . ."

ference between originals and reproductions and their various uses; shows the wide range of the arts by exhibiting examples of architecture, sculpture, painting, glassware, mosaics, ironwork, posters, photography and industrial design, in each case emphasizing how to appreciate such works; demonstrates the formal components of art works, such as plane, line, color, composition, tone, volume and texture; and, finally, demonstrates the use of the various elements of design in the works of some Cuban artists.[60] While for some this may simply be an indication that the sediment of petty-bourgeois culture remains at the bottom of the wine of flourishing revolutionary practice, to other radicals the existence of such a room might well be the acme of revolutionary democracy: making the cultural wealth available to all in a thoughtful, deliberate and meaningful way.

Surely the most vexing problem that faces those who see cultural dissemination, rather than the destruction of culture, as the goal of radical democracy, is the yawning gap which still exists, despite museum programs and articles in the popular media, between art and the public, especially the less-educated and poorer elements of the public. Does anything that happens in the world of art really matter to most people? "There is no use in luring people to museums if they haven't the means of arriving at a true understanding, at a personal experience of works of art," declares André Fermigier. "The majority haven't these means. We find here again our cultural herd. What sight could be more heart-breaking than those haggard crowds that plod through museums, jostling each other in front of the *Mona Lisa* . . . ?"[61]

Already in the nineteenth century, the new mass audience for art was a social phenomenon to be reckoned with. While it may indeed have been true, as Denis Poulot claimed in his prototypical working-class novel, *Le Sublime,* that on Sunday the real worker went for a stroll with his wife and children in the public parks and visited the museums and exhibitions,[62] the lower-class museum-goer seems to have been more bewildered than edified by the cultural riches spread out for his

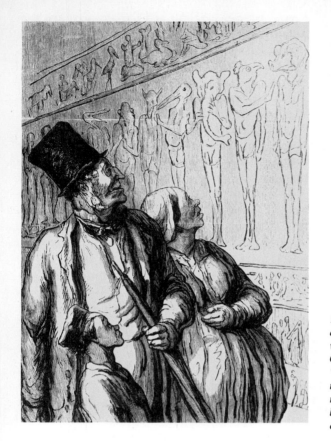

*Honoré Daumier, "The Egyptians
certainly weren't good-looking,"
wood engraving, 1867; Vassar
College, Poughkeepsie, New York.
". . . the lower-class
museum-goer seems to have been
more bewildered than edified
by the cultural riches spread
out for his delectation."*

delectation. "The Egyptians certainly weren't good-looking!" exclaims a modest family before an example of ancient Egyptian wall painting, in Daumier's wood engraving of 1867;[63] and in a lithograph of 1852, a rustic *femme du peuple* and her husband stare up at an amply proportioned nude, while the woman pronounces: "Say, you have to be pretty funny in the head to get your portrait done like that!"[64] In still another lithograph of the same year devoted to "The Public at the Salon," Daumier sympathetically shows the hapless crowd in "A day when you don't have to pay—25 degrees of heat," representing the quite real physical disadvantages attendant upon taking advantage of the free day at the Salon.[65]

There is no more poignant evocation of the un-bridgeable gap between art and the people than the remarkable passage in Zola's *L'Assommoir* where the author describes a visit to the Louvre by the tat-terdamalion wedding party of Gervaise Coupeau, in this novel about the Parisian lower depths during the Second Empire. Certainly, no member of the party had ever been to the museum before, save the cardboard-maker M. Madinier, their cicerone, who knew the place well, since, as he explained, he had been there often with an artist who did designs to put on cardboard boxes. The little group, an amusing spectacle for the artists and regular museum-goers, "trailing all the hand-me-downs of poor people's fashions," trouped dutifully through the endless halls of the great palace of art. They were some-what taken aback by the Assyrian Gallery and thought the statues very ugly: nowadays a good stonecarver could do a lot better job than that. The bareness and severity of the great staircase awed them, as did the magnificent doorkeeper. "It was with great respect, walking as softly as they could, that they entered the French Gallery." Then without pausing, their eyes dazzled by the gold of the frames, they plowed onward through the string of rooms, impressed mainly by the sheer numbers of the works and their valuableness. In the Gallery of Apollo, they were amazed at the sheen of the floor, as shiny as a mir-ror; in the Salon Carré, M. Madinier "murmured un-der his breath, as if he were in church," while some of the less-mannerly wedding guests tittered at the naked women, especially impressed by the thighs of Antiope. More and more pictures! As they struck out through the long gallery with the Italian and Flemish schools, a "jumble of people and things in glaring colors . . . began to give them a headache. . . . Centuries of art passed before their bewildered ig-norance, the fine rigidity of the early Italians, the splendour of the Venetians, the sleek and sunny life of the Dutchman. But what interested them the most were the copyists, with their easels set up in

the midst of the people, painting away undisturbed.
. . . Little by little, the new visitors began to
lose their enthusiasm. . . . The wedding party,
tired out and losing their respect for things, dragged
their hobnailed shoes along, clattering over the
sounding floor with the noise of a herd in confusion,
let loose in the midst of the bare and composed
neatness of the place . . .'' For relief, their guide
led them to Rubens' *Kermesse,* before which the
women screamed and blushed and the men pointed
out the dirty details. Finally, losing their way completely in quest of the collection of ancient jewels,
they blundered in among the drawings: "room
after room with nothing amusing, only bits of paper
covered with scribbles, under glass cases and against
walls.'' At last, in complete rout, lost and terrified,
they found a doorkeeper to "take them in charge and
show them the way to one of the doors. Once in the
courtyard of the Louvre . . . they breathed again.
. . . All the party affected to be very much pleased to
have seen it all.'' [66]

Confusion, awe, misinterpretation, boredom and dis-
orientation—such is the plight of the poor or the
"disadvantaged" in the museum to this very day, if
we are to believe the impressively thorough and
scholarly investigation by the French Centre National
de la Recherche Scientifique, published in Pierre
Bourdieu and Alain Darbel's *L'Amour de l'Art:
Les Musées et Leur Public.*[67] The museums, according to this intra-European investigation, are home
territory only to the more elevated classes of society.
Working-class people, afflicted with what might well
be called "cultural blindness," are often unable to
"decode"—much less appreciate or respond to—the
cherished masterpieces within the sacrosanct walls
of our temples of culture. Two-thirds of the working-
class visitors in the survey were unable to cite, at the
end of their visit, the name of a single work or an
artist that had pleased them; they felt literally lost in

a museum, vaguely dizzy, unable to find their way, fearful of making a false move. Awe was probably the primary "positive" emotion of the uneducated museum-goer, an awe not unmixed with hostility. Seventy-nine percent of the museum-goers of the popular classes associated the museum with the image of a church.[68] It is perhaps no accident that Great Masterpieces of the past should also be associated in the popular mind with the solemn lifelessness of the cemetery: Forest Lawn, with its super-sized Last Supper, its chilly Michelangelos and Donatellos, emitting recorded dirges or commercials for cut-rate interments, its chaste marble nudes and children, carved by certified Florentines and Romans, is far from being a cultural aberration. Rather, it is a potent paradigm of what the popular mind conceives of as Art: something pure and expensive to do with the Dead and Buried, to be visited on Sundays—preferably with organ music in the background.

And lest anyone should think that modernism—i.e., the avant-garde art of the last seventy years or so—has made any headway with the general public in recent times, what with the impact of all the publicity, educational material and the major exhibitions throughout the world devoted to its display and explanation, he or she should direct attention to the sobering—and large-scale—study commissioned by UNESCO's International Council on Museums, published in a recent issue of *Museum*.[69] Conducted in Toronto, Canada, this study, embodying two and a half years' work and combining the skills of museum workers, art historians, social psychologists and market researchers, came up with the startling conclusion that the public simply rejects modern art, in toto. One of the conductors of this survey summarized the findings:

Despite all the claims within the professional communications field . . . that the inventions of the current generation have vastly increased the pace of assimilation of information and the dissemination of knowledge, or of certain artists and critics that, *ergo*, any novelty in art will enjoy rapid acceptance, we can now confidently accept the contrary. As far as art is concerned, the long-observed peculiarity that there exists a generally stable gap of two generations or a minimum of half a century between important creative innovation and its general acceptance by the ordinary public remains true. For all the technical innovations in communications and the vast spread of education, we doubt that the acceptance gap has been shortened by so much as a week. . . . It is not without significance that three of the most violently rejected pictures—by Léger, Feininger, and Mondrian—were all painted in 1917![70]

Among the other definitive findings of this ICOM study, which runs so violently contrary to the hopes and expectations of art educators and museum personnel, as well as those among the ranks of artists themselves who may feel that the great masterpiece will speak directly to some intuitive faculty of the ordinary person, are the following facts: (1) regardless of range of style and expression of the works offered for preference in any given sample of art works, the choice unerringly went to the least radical; (2) there was a consistency in the preference of the test group: 51 percent agreed on the most preferred work, Millet's *Angelus*, and an even higher proportion, 78 percent, agreed on the least preferred work in the sample, Dubuffet's *La Barbe des Incertains Retours*. In addition, the conductors of the survey were "constantly struck by the fact that, despite television, despite picture magazines . . . and other universally available sources of unconscious visual stimulus and education, there is among our respondents a general *lack of ability to recognize a painting as an articulate organization of visual experience if that organization departs very far from traditional forms of visual expression.*"[71]

If one thinks that this conclusion is unwarranted, and that the public could hardly escape being affected by the total impact of the mass media, education and publicity, let me simply present the author's own case: an almost total ignorance of football, which in terms of mass-media bombardment is probably much more widely and forcefully pressed upon me from every side than art information upon the general public. Despite the fact that I have been exposed to football information, seen games in the company of well-liked people under favorable circumstances, as well as over the mass media, since early childhood, have heard the names of famous players, have glanced over articles about the plays, strategy and politics of the game, and while I am vaguely aware that it involves one team (of nine or eleven players, I am not sure) trying to get a ball over the goal post against the counterattack of another team, I may safely say that I have a general lack of ability to recognize the football game as an articulate organization of kinetic experience, and would be completely unable to recognize, much less respond to, innovations in the game, which my informants assure me take place every year. I am, in addition, like the working-class museum-goers in Bourdieu and Darbel's study, totally unable to recall the name of a single football player, after many years of exposure to the game, aside from those of Joe Namath and Knute Rockne, and the two for reasons not directly connected with understanding or appreciation of their worth and prowess as football players. In other words, I am as thoroughly capable of filtering out information which is alien or irrelevant or antipathetic to me as any ordinary museum-goer. And antipathy might well be the key concept in evaluating the public's response to avant-garde art. The gulf between the professional's appreciation of modern art and that of the lay public is not in terms of avoidance of exhibits, but in their attitudes toward them, according to the findings of the ICOM study.[72] For large numbers of people throughout the world, modern art is something to be looked at but hardly enjoyed. "Above all," the study continues:

people resent the unintelligible and even more, what they take to be deliberate efforts on the part of the artists to confuse them. . . . Over and over again [we] encountered the feeling that our respondents were being put-upon by artists who didn't care to be 'understood' by ordinary people . . .[73]

And for those who imagine that some form of "social relevance" in art would, in and of itself, bridge the gap between the ordinary person and modern art, the following findings might be instructive: "References to social problems seem, in their [the respondents'] unarticulated concept of art, to be out of place. Images overtly or otherwise suggestive of catastrophe, human or social decay or other negative aspects of life . . . are viewed as offensive, destructive. What is common-place on TV in the way of violence and other distortions of life is not, in their view, equally acceptable as subject matter for painting''; but lest purists think that art-as-object might be more palatable, the sentence continues, ''but this hardly prepares them to accept non-objective canvases as an alternative: these repel them almost as strongly and, if they get a feeling that the latter 'conceals' the former, the degree of repulsion reaches the greatest extent encountered.''[74]

What is revealed by an examination of the available material on the relation of the public to the museums from the nineteenth century to the present day is that the dimension of art works which sophisticated art historians, critics, avant-garde artists or enlightened museum workers consider ''esthetic'' has generally been irrelevant, incomprehensible or antipathetic to the people as a whole. As Zola noted, ''Room after room with nothing amusing, only bits of papers covered with scribbles . . .''

In the case of radicals' reactions to art, we may remark that the French peasantry vandalized the great cathedrals during the French Revolution not because they objected to the tense linear rhythms or found the style of the Gothic and Romanesque architects distasteful, but because of what these buildings stood for, in social and political rather than esthetic or conventionally iconographic terms; when the Conservatoire of the museum, on 3 Fructidor, Year II, recommended that all the signs of feudalism be effaced by the most skillful restorers from Rubens' Marie de Médicis cycle, the issues involved were hardly esthetic ones, although the committee had the grace to add the rider ''as far as possible, without endangering the works.''[75] Obviously, it is social, psychological and at times political factors that are the determining ones in the attitudes of the public toward what they experience in museums. Nor is the response toward popular or ''admired'' works, like the *Mona Lisa* or Millet's *Angelus*, Murillo's *Flea-Searcher* or Maes's *Old Woman Saying Grace*, necessarily determined by anything like what one might call "esthetic" factors. People respond to something else. The theme of the painting, its age, its fame and the legends about it, its monetary value, its detail, its illusionism, the amount of work that seems to have gone into it—these are the values that count for the general public. And this, of course, is hardly an accidental state of affairs. Art—what is in museums, and especially that created by the self-conscious avant-garde after the middle of the nineteenth century—was rarely intended for the delectation of the vast masses, but rather for a select group of cognoscenti or esthetic sympathizers.

The demand, voiced by advanced artists, ex-artists and new-left radicals, that art "come out of the museums," cease to consist of valuable, market-oriented objects, merge with life—or, in effect, simply disappear—is in many ways an admirable one, and one can, of course, only applaud efforts to get art into the streets and into the lives of ordinary people in the form of community-controlled art projects, wall paintings and workshops. Yet, on the other hand, such demands may simply be the ultimate act of avant-garde, elitist hubris. Once more, the art world tends to over-

Reporters line a ramp in the storage area of the National Gallery of Art in Washington to get a look at Leonardo da Vinci's Mona Lisa, *lent by the Louvre for exhibition in this country in 1963; photo, Associated Press. "... the theme of the painting, its age, its fame and the legends about it, its monetary value, its detail, its illusionism, the amount of work that seems to have gone into it—these are the values that count for the general public."*

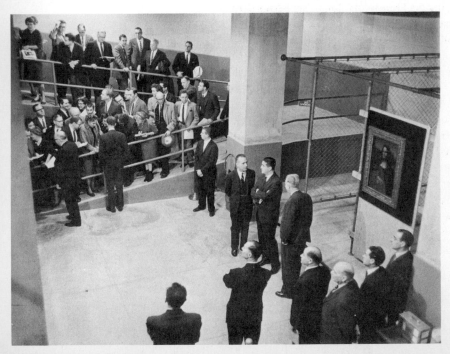

estimate the power and range of its productions and its actions by imagining the drastic effect that the disappearance of all those canvas rectangles would have on the social system. The death of art? The destruction of culture? The demise of the museum? These phrases tend to ring hollow: for the vast majority of people throughout the world, struggling against poverty, decimated by war and hunger or crushed by demeaning life-styles, neither art nor culture nor the museums themselves have ever really been alive.

---

1. I should like to thank Susan Bainbridge, Rosalind Leech and Marilyn Sims, my students at Vassar College, as well as Alison Hilton, a Ph.D. candidate at Columbia University, for their invaluable assistance in the research for this article. Susan Casteras also helped in its preparation, as did Edith Tonelli.

2. While there were certain collections open to the public on a restricted basis, which might be said to have had precedence over the Louvre in the eighteenth century—i.e., the Vatican Museums, those of Florence and Dresden, the British Museum, as well as the Gemäldegalerie at Kassel—in general, the principle of public control over and free access to art and art collections was not fully applied until the opening of the Louvre in 1793. For information about the evolution of the concept of the museum in the eighteenth century, see: L. Salerno, "Museums and Collections," *Encyclopedia of World Art* (New York: McGraw-Hill, 1965), vol. 10, p. 390; H. Seling, "The Genesis of the Museum," *The Architectural Review,* vol. 141, No. 840 (February 1967): pp. 103–114; and V. Plagemann, *Das deutsche Kunstmuseum 1790–1870* (Munich, 1967), pp. 11–21. For the history of the Louvre as a museum, see especially: C. Aulanier, *Histoire du Palais et du Musée de Louvre* (Paris, n.d.), and L. Hautecoeur, *Histoire du Louvre: Le Chateau —Le Palais—Le Musée* (Paris, n.d.), pp.77–109.

3. Implicit to the "democratic" view of the museum is, of course, the notion that there is such a thing as art, that this art consists of certain classes of objects rather than others, and that confrontation of these objects, knowledge of their history, and enjoyment or appreciation of their quality are unquestionably good for the general public—a view certainly *not* shared by such eminent thinkers as Plato or Tolstoy, although taken for granted by most art workers.

4. At least for three days out of every ten, the first five days being reserved for artists, the next two for cleaning and arranging. It was not until a year later that it was decided that the museum should be open every day to the general public. See M. Dreyfous, *Les Arts et les Artistes pendant la Période Révolutionnaire* (Paris, [1916]), p. 77.

5. C. Gould, *Trophy of Conquest: The Musée Napoléon and the Creation of the Louvre* (London, 1965), p.28.

6. B. St. John, *The Louvre: Biography of a Museum* (London, 1855), p.57.

7. For Lenoir's own views on his Museum of French Monuments, as well as those of a visitor, see L. Eitner, *Neoclassicism and Romanticism, 1750–1850* (Englewood Cliffs, 1970), vol. 2, pp.5–7.

8. Napoleon had very little interest in, or understanding of, the visual arts *per se*, quite simply viewing the works of art he "liberated" as trophies of war.

9. Gould, op. cit., p.32.

10. Ibid, pp.35–36.

11. Dreyfous, op. cit., pp.73–74.

12. Gould, op. cit., p.49.

13. Lord Elgin certainly used this excuse for carrying off the Parthenon sculptures, which he, and his supporters, with a good deal of justification, considered a salvaging rather than a looting operation. The destruction of "the ruin of the noblest works of art in the world" had been "progressing with giant steps" at the time Lord Elgin undertook his mission, according to the *Report from the Select Committee on the Earl of Elgin's Collection of Marbles*, etc. See F. H. Taylor, *The Taste of Angels* (Boston, 1948), p. 498. Nevertheless, his opponents, among them Lord Byron, accused him of pillaging Greece for profit. Childe Harold laments: "Thy walls defaced, thy mould'ring shrines removed / By British hands which it had best behoved / To guard those relics ne'er to be restored . . ." Ibid., p. 504.

14. Gould, op. cit., p.68.

15. Taylor, op. cit., p.578.

16. St. John, op. cit., pp.71–72.

17. Taylor, op. cit., p.578.

18. H. B. Stowe, *Sunny Memories of Foreign Lands* (Boston, 1854), vol. 2, pp.170–72.

19. Eitner, op. cit., vol. 1, pp.140–41.

20. A. Lenoir in Eitner, op. cit., vol. 2, p.5.

21. For examples of revolutionary vandalism and steps taken against it by the revolutionary government, see Dreyfous, op. cit., pp.3–29.

22. *Moniteur Universel*, April 29, 1848, p.909.

23. Among his works with proletarian sympathies and subjects were *Les Forgerons de la Corrèze* of 1836, praised by the critic Théophile Thoré as the first step toward a new, popular art, and *The Little Patriots: A Souvenir of July 1830*, a scene from the revolution of that year.

24. S. Meltzoff, "The Revival of the Le Nains," *The Art Bulletin*, vol. 24 (1942), pp.264–65.

25. St. John, op. cit., p.278.

26. *Moniteur Universel*, April 11, 1848, pp. 808–09.

27. G. Mack, *Gustave Courbet*, (New York, 1951), p.243.

28. Cited in G. Darcel, "Les Musées, Les Arts et les

Artistes pendant la Commune,'' *Gazette des Beaux-Arts,* vol. 5 (1872), p.46.

29. G. Courbet, cited in Darcel, loc. cit.

30. Cited in Darcel, op. cit., pp.48–49.

31. Cited ibid., p.480.

32. R. Moulin, "Living without Selling," *Art and Confrontation: The Arts in an Age of Change,* trans. N. Foxell (New York, 1968), p.133.

33. Ibid., pp.133–34.

34. T. Reff, "Copyists in the Louvre, 1850-1870," *The Art Bulletin,* vol. 46 (1964), p.553.

35. Reff, loc. cit.

36. F. T. Marinetti in "The Foundation and Manifesto of Futurism," 1908, in H. B. Chipp, *Theories of Modern Art: A Source Book by Artists and Critics* (Berkeley and Los Angeles, 1969), p.288.

37. Cited by Reff, op. cit., n. 5, p.553. The issue of Louvre-burning was brought to its ultimate conclusion by the editors of *L'Esprit Nouveau* in about 1920, when they published a series of answers to the question: "Faut-il brûler le Louvre?" Their respondents were about equally divided on the question. See "Faut-il brûler le Louvre?" *L'Esprit Nouveau,* No. 6, n.d., after p.718 (pp.1–8) and No. 8, n.d., pp.960-62.

38. Later, he told Mary Cassatt that he didn't have time to go to the Louvre, and there is no record of his ever having copied there (Reff, loc. cit.). Also see the exhibition catalogue *Claude Monet,* Arts Council of Great Britain, Tate Gallery, 1957, p.8.

39. Chipp, op. cit., p.286.

40. Ibid., p.287. The image of the museum as a cemetery achieved ample realization, in reverse, in the great American rural cemeteries of the nineteenth century, which were really outdoor sculpture museums, as were, and are, many European cemeteries of the period: in many cases, in our country, the cemetery was the only place where "high art" was readily available, and the cemetery-as-museum finds its apotheosis in that vast outdoor shrine of kitsch culture, Forest Lawn. The museum-cemetery image has even been used, with slight variation, by those who see the culture of the past as worth protecting, like Etienne Gilson, who defined the general art museum by stating that "museums provide homes for aged masterpieces." Cited by E. B. Henning, *Art Journal,* vol. 30 (Fall 1970): vol. 30, no. 1, p.21. The distance from the old age home to the grave is not enormous.

41. For further information about radicals and art, especially in France and Belgium, see E. W. Herbert, *The Artist and Social Reform: France and Belgium, 1885–1898* (New Haven, 1961), and R. L. and E. W. Herbert, "Artists and Anarchism: Unpublished Letters of Pissarro, Signac, and Others," *Burlington Magazine,* vol. 102 (1960), Part 1, pp.473–82, Part 2, pp.517–22.

42. Cited in C. H. Gibbs-Smith and K. Dougharty, *The*

History of the Victoria and Albert Museum, Small Picture Book No. 31 (London, 1952), p.5.

43. Ibid., p.6.

44. Cited in Q. Bell, *The Schools of Design* (London, 1963), pp.166–67.

45. C. P. Taft, *Lecture on the South Kensington Museum: What it is; How it originated; What it has done and is now doing for England and the World; and the Adaptation of such an Institution to the Needs and Possibilities of Cincinnati* (Cincinnati, 1878), p.10.

46. W. Morris, from a lecture, *The Lesser Arts*, 1878, in *William Morris: Selected Writings and Designs*, ed. A. Briggs (Baltimore, 1962), pp.95–96.

47. Ibid., pp.103-04.

48. Morris, loc. cit.

49. W. Morris, *News from Nowhere*, 1890, in *William Morris: Selected Writings*, p.220.

50. Ibid., p.299.

51. E. Lissitzky, *Life–Letters–Texts*, ed. S. Lissitzky-Küppers, trans. H. Aldwinckle (London, 1968), p.330. Interestingly enough, El Lissitzky himself created a new and revolutionary gallery in the Hanover Museum for a display of abstract painting in 1929. It consisted of insubstantial walls with vertical iron strips ranged against them throwing "clefts of shadow and dematerializ[ing] the wall to the point where it seems to dissolve completely," according to Sigfried Giedion in an article praising the gallery at the time. As Giedion pointed out, Lissitzky's gallery proved "that museums need not be mausoleums . . ." S. Giedion in Lissitzky, op. cit., p.379.

52. Cited in R. Hunt, "The Constructivist Ethos: Russia 1913–1932" (Part 2), *Artforum*, vol. 6 (October, 1967), p.28.

53. Cited in R. Hunt, "The Constructivist Ethos: Russia 1913–1932 (Part 1), *Artforum*, vol. 6 (September, 1967), p.24.

54. Ibid., p.28.

55. Cited in Hunt, loc. cit.

56. Lissitzky, op. cit., p.337.

57. M. Ragon, "The Artist and Society: Rejection or Integration," *Art and Confrontation* (see ref. 32), p.37.

58. See S. Sontag, "The Cuban Poster," *Artforum*, vol. 9 (October, 1970), pp.56–63. For reproductions of Cuban posters, see D. Stermer, *The Art of Revolution* (New York, 1970).

59. "Art Education Room in the National Museum of Cuba, Havana," *Museum*, vol. 22, No. 3/4 (1969), pp.222–225. The rationale behind this room is strikingly similar to the proposal for didactic museum organization made by John Berger in 1966: "The Historical Function of the Museum," *The Moment of Cubism and Other Essays* (London, 1969), pp.35–40.

60. "Art Education Room," op. cit., passim.

61. A. Fermigier, "'No More Claudels,'" *Art and Confrontation* (see ref. 32), pp.58–59.

62. Cited in notes to E. Zola, *L'Assommoir*, in A. Lanoux,

ed., *Les Rougon-Macquart* (Paris, Pléiade, 1961), p.1579.

63. The wood engraving was one of a series satirizing the Universal Exposition of 1867 that Daumier did for *Le Monde Illustré* in 1867–68. The work appeared on Oct. 26, 1867, Rühman Cat. No. 893, Boury Cat. No. 949.

64. Delteil No. 2298.

65. Delteil No. 2300.

66. E. Zola, *The Drunkard (L'Assommoir),* trans. A. Symons (London, 1958), pp. 75–81, passim.

67. This brilliant, methodologically rigorous study included samples from a cross-section of museums in France and will eventually incorporate data obtained by research teams in Spain, Greece, Italy, the Low Countries and Poland. See P. Bourdieu and A. Darbel, *L'Amour de l'Art: Les Musées et Leur Public* (Paris, 1966).

68. Ibid., p. 74.

69. A. Zacks, D. F. Cameron, D. S. Abbey, et al., "Public Attitudes toward Modern Art," *Museum,* vol. 22, No. 3/4 (1969), pp.125–80.

70. T. A. Heinrich in op. cit., p. 140.

71. Ibid., p.142.

72. D. S. Abbey in op. cit., p.134.

73. T. A. Heinrich in op. cit., p.143.

74. Ibid., p.144.

75. Dreyfous, op. cit., p. 72.

The failed Utopia: Russian art 1917–32

JOHN E. BOWLT

"The Revolution of October 1917 reverberated through
all sections of Russian society. In the field of
art its immediate effect was to alter the artist's
social position—a change which, in turn,
profoundly influenced the direction of his creative
output. Suddenly the artist assumed bureaucratic
and administrative responsibilities which previously
he had scarcely experienced, and it was
this in particular which contributed to the dynamic
but short-lived dictatorship of the left in art."

Before 1917 the so-called "leftist" artists had led an underground existence spiritually alien to the mainstream of bourgeois society. This position was clearly demonstrated in the choice of name for the avant-garde group the "Knave of Diamonds" (1910–25), chosen, according to one source, because Czarist prison uniforms carried such shapes—an association which was very much to the taste of the new artistic outcasts.[1] Materially, the leftist artists had relied to a marked extent on private patronage—a tradition which went back at least as far as P. V. Tretyakov (1832–1898) and S. I. Mamontov (1841–1918). During the 1900s the powerful merchant family of the Ryabushinskys, especially Nikolai Pavlovich, was particularly active in this area, not only in purchasing works but also in financing exhibitions and publications. During the years of artistic extremism after 1910 other figures achieved recognition as art patrons, notably N. I. Kulbin (1866–1917), L. I. Zheverzheev (1881–1942) and several wealthy members of the Moscow Society of Free Esthetics, but they were selective in their purchases and tended to neglect the most dynamic artists, such as N. S. Goncharova (1881–1962), M. F. Larionov (1881–1964), K. S. Malevich (1878–1935) and V. E. Tatlin (1885–1953).[2] To a certain extent it was private finance which contributed to the "boom" in artistic activity just before the Revolution both in theoretical formulation and in creative achievement, and certain important groups, among them the Union of Youth (1910–14), owed their existence to donations of this sort. Such groups, of course, served as platforms for attacks on conventional art and society at large, and widened still further the gap between the cultural avant-garde and the Establishment. It was this gap between the artist and society which the Revolution attempted to overcome.

After the October Revolution the artist's dependence on private finance was replaced by state patronage and his leftism was officially recognized. Once outlawed, he was now regarded as a fellow traveler, even as the herald of Socialist Revolution, for the broken forms of his Cubo-Futurism and Suprematism were seen as the description of a dying bourgeois order; this concept

was shared by many prominent artists and evidently inspired Malevich, for example, to declare that "Cubism
and Futurism were revolutionary movements in art
anticipating the revolution in the economic and political
life of 1917."[3] As cultural revolutionaries, the leftists
emerged as champions of the new society and were
treated as such, at least initially, by being awarded positions of authority in all walks of artistic life. At the same
time, because of the government's concentration on the
burning issues of the day—civil war, famine, rapid
industrialization—official policies affecting the visual
arts tended to be obscure and difficult to implement. It
was therefore with relative ease that leftist artists took
up important appointments, both at a practical level as
in the state art schools and at an organizational one in
the bureaucratic hierarchy.

It should be stressed, however, that the Party did
have at least a tentative scheme for the organization
and manipulation of a distinct, mass culture, a program
which Lenin had outlined as early as 1905.[4] The various
Party declarations of late 1917 and onward, on the role
of art in a Socialist society, did follow a certain pattern,
the significance of which is quite apparent in the following statement of December 1917 by the Central
Committee: "In art the proletariat . . . considers near
to him that which is expressed in strong, vivid and
definite forms, that which is complete and has distinct
meaning."[5] But the lack of direct Party control over
the arts, the lack of doctrinal communication between
politicians and artists as well as the Party's concern
with more immediate problems, contributed to the neglect of its own cultural interpretations and to the domina-
tion of the left. Indeed, it seemed to contemporary observers that the Party itself had little sense of artistic
direction, a conviction which caused the art critic A.M.
Efros (1888–1954) to write in 1922: "The new State
did not have its own artistic tastes or programs; by up-
bringing the leaders of political power were attracted
to the Wanderers; in any case, they went no further
than that popular, imitative Impressionism by which
the Union of Russian Artists had earned its living."[6]
The conservative artistic inclinations of the political

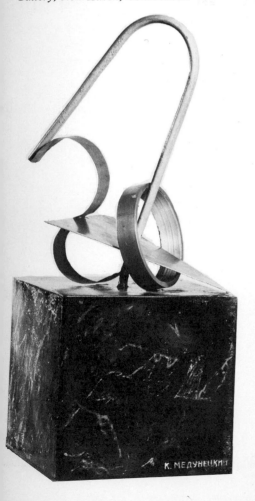

Kasimir Medunetsky, Construction
No. 557, *tin, brass and iron,*
1919; Yale University Art
Gallery, New Haven, Connecticut.

leaders, including Lenin, tended to emphasize the distance between the Party machine and the leftist artists, even though the revolutionary fervor of the latter was regarded as a postive contribution to the new regime.

The fundamental changes which transformed the art world after October 1917 were, to a certain extent, anticipated earlier that year immediately after the political disorders of February. The shootings and demonstrations of that month disturbed the tenor of artistic life; many artists, especially in the urban centers, suddenly gained political consciousness. This was reflected not only in a renewed attention to the poster and newspaper caricature as art forms (which had achieved popularity during the 1905 revolution), but also in a move toward administrative and agitational activity. Artists, aware of their own fragmentation, attempted to unite their many factions under the umbrella of large unions such as the Petrograd Union of Art Workers and the Council of Organizations of Moscow Artists. In addition, committees were founded to attend to the problem of preserving abandoned palaces and works of art and to achieve a rapprochement between artists and ordinary workers.

It is significant to discover that Malevich and G. B. Yakulov (1884–1928) were among the radical artists attached to the Moscow Council of Soldiers' Deputies established just after February. Of the many similar enterprises this was one of the most successful in the dissemination of art among the masses. It even published its own journal, the *Path of Liberation,* to which soldier-artists were encouraged to contribute; apart from this it organized lectures and invited would-be artists, too poor to afford tuition, to attend open days at professional studios. Many other important artists were active in this area, including P. P. Konchalovsky (1876–1956), P. V. Kuznetsov (1878–1968), K. S. Petrov-Vodkin (1878–1939), I. I. Mashkov (1881–1944) and Tatlin. In this way prominent artists formed an alliance with the masses and gained valuable organizational experience which prepared them for their administrative tasks after October.

Immediately after the Revolution the traditional bureaucracy which had controlled art education (including the St. Petersburg Academy of Arts, galleries, museums, exhibitions, etc.) was abolished and replaced by Narkompros (abbreviation of People's Commissariat for Enlightenment). It was the establishment of Narkompros, the presence of the Proletkult network (abbreviation of Proletarian Culture), the formation of Inkhuk (abbreviation of Institute of Artistic Culture) and the complete reorganization of art schools which afforded the artist unprecedented opportunities to wield administrative and bureaucratic power and so to propagate his own private beliefs. At first centered on Petrograd, before the capital was transferred to Moscow, Narkompros was controlled by the Commissar for Enlightenment, A. V. Lunacharsky (1875–1933), whose liberal views stimulated leftist activity at least during the early years. Although from the very beginning Narkompros contained an art section, this was expanded in April 1918 to become IZO (abbreviation of Department of Visual Arts); this, in turn, was divided into two subsections, or collegiates, which became responsible for Petrograd and Moscow respectively, and separate IZOs were established in provincial centers.

One of the important results of these innovations was that they introduced leftist artists into the hierarchy of administration: D. V. Shterenberg (1881–1948) was appointed head of the Petrograd collegiate, Tatlin head of the Moscow one, and they were quickly joined by such progressive figures as N. I. Altman (1889–1970) and N. N. Punin (1888–1953) in Petrograd, R.R. Falk (1886–1958) and Malevich in Moscow. The question immediately arises as to why such extremists were chosen for key administrative posts. To answer this several important circumstances must be referred to: first, Lunacharsky was very close to the leftists both in art and in literature and recommended certain of their names to Lenin; second, the pre-Revolutionary Cubo-Futurists and Suprematists had learned methods of organization and manipulation from their own intense activity (the proclamation of manifestos, the opening of exhibitions, the formation of groups, the staging of

Alexander Rodchenko, Composition, woodcut, 1919; Hutton-Hutschnecker Gallery, New York.

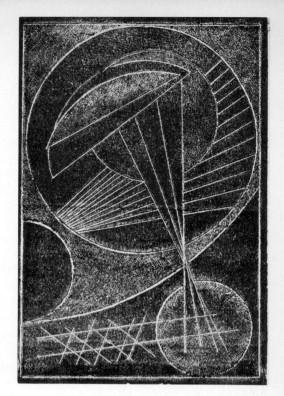

I. Kudryashev, Mural design for the auditorium in the First Soviet Theater, Orenburg, 1920; Tretyakov Gallery, Moscow.

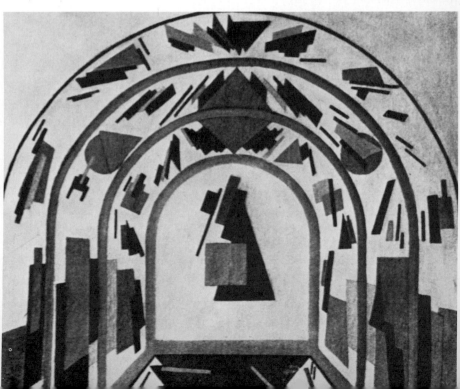

public debates, etc.); third, the ranks of the avant-garde were swelled by the return of émigré colleagues to Russia (such as Chagall—in 1914—Gabo, Kandinsky, Pevsner, Shterenberg); fourth, obvious choices for administrative posts, such as A. N. Benois (1870–1960) and I. E. Grabar (1871–1960) who were professional critics and museum workers as well as painters, were absorbed into the Department of Museums and Preservation of Artistic Monuments, where all their energies and talents were necessarily devoted to restoration, cataloguing of requisitioned private collections and museum reorganization.

As a result, many of the pre-Revolutionary leftists became associated with Narkompros either in an administrative or in an advisory capacity. Kandinsky, for example, helped to establish Inkhuk in 1920, M. V. Matyushin (1861–1934) played an important role in the reconstruction of the Academy of Arts, and O. V. Rozanova (1886–1918) was instrumental in the formation of a Department of Industrial Art within Narkompros. It was natural, therefore, that Narkompros should have recommended the purchase of leftist works for the reserves of state museums, and items of A. V. Lentulov (1882–1943), Malevich, Pevsner, Tatlin, et al. were, in fact, bought officially. In addition, large-scale exhibitions were sponsored, including the famous sixteen state exhibitions of 1918 and 1919 and the Berlin exhibition of 1922. The progressive attitude of Narkompros in the early years was epitomized by Malevich's ten commandments for a comprehensive State art policy: "(1) War on academism . . . (3) The creation of a worldwide collective for art affairs . . . (4) The establishment of art embassies in foreign countries . . . (10) The publication of a newspaper on questions of art for the public at large."[7]

Art critics such as O. M. Brik (1888–1945) and Punin occupied influential posts within the structure of Narkompros and contributed to the cause of leftism particularly by their articles in the journals *Art of the Commune* (Petrograd, 1918–19), *Visual Art* (Petrograd, 1919) and *Lef/New Lef* (Moscow, 1923–25, 1927–28). These publications advocated Futurism or Communist

Futurism and, later, Constructivism (in *Lef*) as art forms essential to the new proletarian order and resisted any return to Realism: "A Communist regime demands a Communist consciousness. All forms of life, morality, philosophy and art must be re-created according to Communist principles. . . . In their activities the cultural-educational organs of the Soviet government show a complete misunderstanding of the revolutionary task entrusted to them. . . . Under the guise of immutable truths the masses are being presented with the pseudo-teachings of the gentry."[8]

The above criticism was directed not only at the "representational" tastes of the political leaders, but also at their initial expenditure on the preservation of historic monuments, an act which many leftists considered retrograde. This view was identifiable, above all, with the Proletkult organization. Significantly, Proletkult had emerged as an effective body as early as February 1917, when it had attempted to form a closer association between artists and workers, although it was not inaugurated officially until September of that year. Headed by A. A. Bogdanov (1873–1928), Proletkult maintained that a proletarian art could be realized only by the proletariat itself and that the legacy of bourgeois culture was, for the most part, unnecessary and irrelevant—a position that inspired such slogans as "In the name of our tomorrow, let us burn Raphael."[9]

Although the autonomy of Proletkult was soon threatened by the Party and considerably weakened thereby in 1921, it anticipated the movement toward industrial art and Constructivism; in declaring that the new art should be a proletarian one, it directed attention to the factory and the machine. As early as August 1918, in fact, Rozanova was appointed head of a Department of Art-Production within Proletkult, and by 1920 it contained a network of over a hundred affiliates in urban centers. The activities of Proletkult worried Lenin, however, and by the autumn of 1918 he was openly critical of it despite the support of Lunacharsky and Shterenberg. In December 1920 the Party officially condemned Proletkult, mainly because of its independence of the political hierarchy: "Thanks to this and many other reasons, elements socially alien to us have swept into Proletkult . . . and in the sphere of art they have injected the workers with absurd, perverted tastes (Futurism)."[10] The significance of this decree lay not only in its formal condemnation of the Proletkult organization, but also in its overt criticism of Futurism, for by then the word Futurism was already being used as a blanket term for non-Realism.

The Party's attitude toward the concepts of Realism and Classicism was not, however, definite during the early years. On the one hand it took measures to preserve the bourgeois past, as in the establishment of the Narkompros Museum Department (November 1917); on the other it encouraged the destruction of Russia's cultural heritage, as in the famous decree on Monumental Propaganda (April 1918). Lenin's position in this context was undoubtedly on the side of preservation, and, indeed, his opinion had always been that a new, proletarian culture must be founded on the assimilation of the best artistic traditions of the feudal and capitalist past: "Why do we have to turn away from the truly beautiful, reject it as a starting point for further development merely on the basis that it is 'old'? Why do we have to worship the new, like a 'god' whom we have to submit to simply because 'it is new'? . . . I just cannot consider the works of Expressionism, Futurism, Cubism and other 'isms' as the highest manifestation of artistic genius. I do not understand them. I do not experience any pleasure from them."[11]

Ironically, it was the plan of Monumental Propaganda formulated by Lenin and Lunacharsky which further disseminated Cubo-Futurist and abstractionist ideas among the masses. The decree requested that the Czarist monuments of no "artistic" or "historic" interest be demolished and that temporary or permanent monuments to the outstanding revolutionaries and liberators of mankind be erected in their place, preferably in time for the May Day celebrations;[12] in addition, the mass decoration of streets and squares was advocated—a measure which was soon extended to include the so-called agit-trains, agit-steamers and agit-cars. Despite objections by such figures as Shterenberg and Tatlin that the plan was financially impracticable, artistically questionable and doomed to failure because the country lacked sufficient numbers of monumental artists, many leftist sculptors and painters submitted designs; this led directly to the construction of the Cubo-Futurist statue to Bakunin by B. D. Korolev (1885–1963) in Moscow and Altman's decoration for Uritsky Square, Petrograd. Other contributors to street decoration included A.V. Kuprin (1880–1960), Lentulov, Petrov-Vodkin and Shterenberg. Yet, while providing an extraordinary opportunity for creative experiment in a relatively untested medium, banner, billboard and poster art as produced by the avant-garde encountered hostility from the general public, for the new spectator was unused to the excesses of Cubo-Futurism and demanded an art

El Lissitzky, Proun, *two-color lithograph with collage, 1919–23; Museum of Modern Art, New York.*

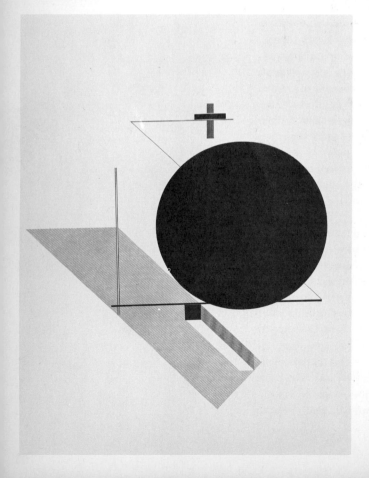

intelligible and emotive; in some cases workers' reaction resulted in monuments being dismantled and decorations being torn down. Describing the Bakunin statue under the title "Clear Away the Scarecrow," one indignant worker wrote: "The statue is not exactly just a narrow slab of stone, and it's not exactly the remains of some kind of ugly tree, but one thing's certain—it's a scarecrow very much resembling a man. . . . Workers and Red Army men . . . are surprised and outraged when they find out that the monument is about to be unveiled."[13]

Chagall has left us the description of a similar reaction by Party officials to the decorations executed by him and his pupils for Vitebsk: "Why is the cow green and why is the horse flying in the sky? Why? What has that to do with Marx and Lenin?"[14] The political response to this situation was that Narkompros was openly criticized for tolerating Futurism on such a wide scale, and by the spring of 1919, when similar arrangements were envisaged for new May Day festivities, Futurists in Petrograd were refused orders for street decoration. Similarly, a new commission was established, under the more moderate artist I. I. Nivinsky (1880–1933), to control extremism in design for agit-transport. After this date orders for decoration came to be fulfilled increasingly by representationalists, some of whom, however, such as D. S. Moor (1883–1946) and A. A. Radakov (1879–1942), won justifiable praise both in their broadly appealing simplistic themes and in their artistic treatment.

Perhaps the most positive result of the move toward agit-art in 1918 was the stimulus it provided for easel painters to turn from "art for art's sake" to applied art—a development inspired also by the Proletkult drive for a proletarian art founded on industrial production and by the general awareness of abstract painters that easel painting had run its course. In turn, of course, this assisted the emergence of Constructivism, with its emphasis on "extra-artistic" elements, on functionalism and on machine art. Applied art soon came to affect many facets of Soviet life—from clothes (A. A. Exter, 1884–1949) to the theater (L. S. Popova, 1889–1924), from stamps (Altman) to porcelain (Kandinsky, Malevich), from book covers and photography (El Lissitzky, 1890–1941, A. M Rodchenko, 1891–1956) to furniture (N. M. Suetin, 1897–1954)—in design that often contained the ingredients of Cubo-Futurist or Suprematist easel painting.

It should be observed that the presence of such styles contributed to the generalization of Constructivist principles. To a certain extent Constructivism in its initial, purist phase provided a solution to the problem of eclecticism which was besieging Soviet art under the liberal policies of Narkompros. Its concentration on "modern materials" and on rationality was, of course, exemplified, somewhat prematurely, by Tatlin's model for the Tower to the Third International (1919); also by the free-standing constructions of members of the Obmokhu[15] group such as K. K. Medunetsky (b. 1899) and Rodchenko. But despite the exhibitions, debates and manifestos associated with the first Constructivists, including the famous but perhaps overrated Realistic Manifesto of Gabo and Pevsner (August 1920), their works evoked criticism by the public at large: "Every morning . . . I see a group of locals who stand in hostile surprise in front of a window with the loud title 'Obmokhu.' . . . The window further proclaims: 'Art is the wheelbarrow which delivers everyone from the pregnancy of stupidity. . . . Our duty is to put on the yoke of art in order to take off the hemorrhoids of the brain,' etc. Now I understand the hostile surprise of the locals and the surprise and indignation of the workers who are forced to look at this public indecency and mockery of common sense. And these are young artists! Perhaps you'll even say this is proletarian art? No, a thousand times no!"[16] The general public reaction to such works of Constructivism echoed throughout the Party echelons, and serious doubt was expressed on the relevance of such art to a Socialist society.

The formation of Inkhuk in May 1920 and its subsequent activities contributed significantly to the practice of Constructivism in the early 1920s, even though

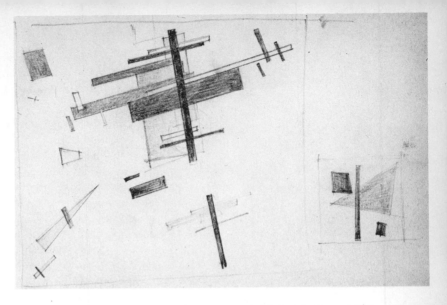

Kasimir Malevich, Suprematist Architectural Drawing, *pencil, 1922; Hutton-Hutschnecker Gallery, New York.*

the Institute partially lost identity when fused with the Academy of Sciences in 1922. Inkhuk was based in Moscow initially under Kandinsky, and it had subsidiaries in Petrograd (controlled by Punin and Tatlin) and Vitebsk (controlled by Malevich). The main function of Inkhuk was to reduce the principal modern movements to a scientific discipline, and Kandinsky formulated a program to cover Suprematism, Colorism and the "culture of materials," a program which was not, however, accepted by the majority (his disagreements with his colleagues over this led to his resignation at the end of 1920). At Inkhuk experiments were carried out on the material properties of paint, on the psychological effects of color, on the interrelationships of color and sound—experiments which produced the term "laboratory art." Members of Inkhuk, among them A. D. Drevin (1889–1938), I. V. Klyun (1870–1942), Malevich, Rodchenko, Tatlin, N. A. Udaltsova (1886–1961), incorporated the results of "laboratory art" into their works, although many projects remained unrealized because of an acute shortage of materials. In November 1921 Inkhuk suffered an internal rift thanks to the total rejection of easel painting by Popova, Rodchenko, V. F. Stepanova (1894-1958), et al. and their immediate departure into industrial design and photography; two months later Inkhuk as such was

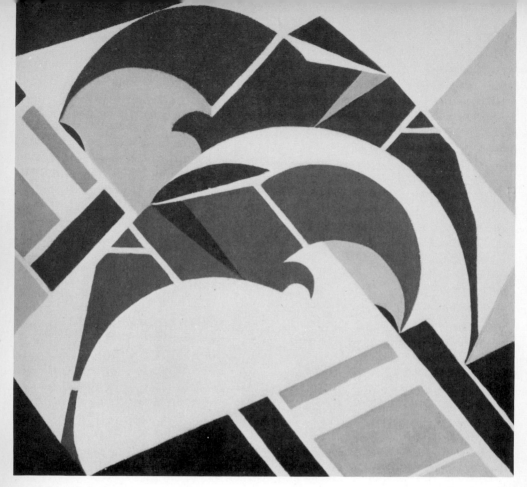

Alexander Rodchenko,
Untitled, *oil,*
c. 1918; Galerie
Jean Chauvelin, Paris.

reorganized—an event symptomatic of the crisis which leftist art was about to enter.

Probably the most radical and far-reaching transformation which took place under Narkompros was the reorganization of the art schools. In April 1918, the old St. Petersburg Academy was abolished and replaced by Svomas (abbreviation of Free Art Studios), which subsequently were replaced in 1921 by the restored Academy. Also during 1918, the old Moscow Institute of Painting, Sculpture and Architecture was combined with the Stroganov Institute to form a second complex of Svomas; these in 1920 were renamed Vkhutemas (which is an abbreviation of Higher State Art-Technical Studios).[17] Changes were felt particularly in the sphere of instruction: the entrance examination was abolished, students were allowed to choose their own teachers and courses, study of art history was optional. Such a liberal program enabled many leftists to take up teaching posts both at the metropolitan art schools and in the provincial institutes which were reorganized on similar lines. Altman, Matyushin, Pougny, Tatlin taught at Svomas in Petrograd; Drevin, Klyun, Malevich, Shevchenko taught at Svomas/Vkhutemas in Moscow; Chagall headed the art school in Vitebsk.[18] The painter A. A. Rylov (1870–1939) later recalled the position at the Petrograd Svomas: "More than fifteen individual studios of all possible trends had opened [in 1918]: extreme 'leftism' was especially noticeable in the studios of Professor Tatlin under the sign 'Construction, Volume and Material' and Professor Matyushin with his theory of 'Extended Viewing.' In Tatlin's studio there was an anvil, a carpenter's bench, a lathe, etc., instead of easels . . ."[19]

But while these art schools acted as platforms for advocating the artistic ideas of Malevich, Rodchenko, Tatlin, etc., they served also as targets for dissent and dissatisfaction with Cubo-Futurist or abstractionist disciplines. Certainly, the avant-garde studios did produce some disciples, such as I. Kudryashev (Koudriachov, b. 1896), I. G. Chashnik (1902–1929)—both under Malevich—and T. M. Shapiro—under Tatlin—but many students decisively reacted against them and either left the art schools or turned to Realism as an artistic credo. As early as November 1920 a group of students at the Moscow Svomas complained to Lunacharsky of the Futurist monopoly at the school and requested that they be authorized to invite Realists as permanent instructors.[20] This shift in artistic direction was accelerated by the establishment of AKhRR (abbreviation of Association of Artists of Revolutionary Russia)[21] in 1922, a Realist organization which immediately won Party approval by its endeavors to depict topical, intelligible scenes. Soon there followed a host of other representational groups, such as OST (Society of Easel Painters), NOZh (New Society of Painters) and "4 Arts," which presented a serious threat to abstract development and undoubtedly influenced educational policy.

It is important to bear in mind that the move back to Realism in the 1920s was the result not only of political pressure, but also of personal, artistic conviction. In this respect the declaration of NOZh in 1922, signed by former pupils of Exter, Malevich and Tatlin, pointed to the way in which Soviet art would evolve; "We, former leftists in art, were the first to feel the utter rootlessness of further analytical, scholastic meanderings going further and further away from life and art . . . we have not followed the path trodden by the theory of Constructivism, for Constructivism in pro-

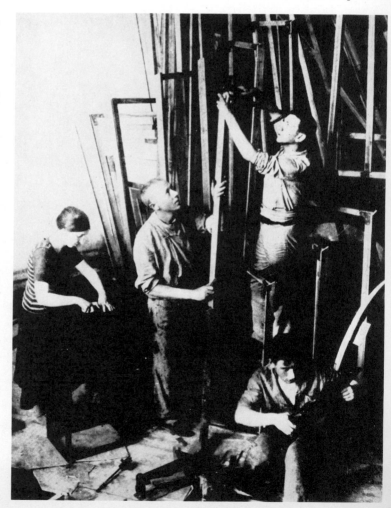

In a 1919, post-Revolution photo, Vladimir Tatlin (second from left) works on a model of his proposed Monument for the Third International; he is aided by S. Tolstaya, his disciple T. M. Shapiro, and by I. Meierzon (foreground). The spiraled metal tower, planned to surpass the Eiffel Tower—at 1,300 feet— was actually never built.

claiming death to art conceives Man as an automaton . . . we wish to create real works of art.''[22] The ''real works of art'' were readily appreciated by the Party, the public at large and, specifically, by the new, private customer who had appeared as a result of NEP (New Economic Policy). This new middle class fought shy of artistic extremism and favored an art that was immediately intelligible, and therefore provided important, material support for the expanding movement of Realist painters. Significantly, several members of the ''Knave of Diamonds'' group renounced ''formalism'' and turned to Realism: Mashkov joined AKhRR in 1924, Falk and Lentulov joined it in 1926; other leftists, such as L. A. Bruni (1894–1948), Drevin and Udaltsova, dismissed abstraction and approached Realism by way of Expressionism and Symbolism.

As Stalin came to dominate the total political arena, the Party began increasingly to interfere in matters of culture, particularly after the decree of 1925, ''On the Party's Policy in the Field of Artistic Literature,'' which emphasized the socially tendentious role which art should play. Of course, some artistic experimentation continued throughout the mid- and late 1920s, even though the leftist was again being driven underground. Interesting developments took place especially on the international front. In 1927 Malevich visited Lodz and Berlin, in 1928 Lissitzky returned from his sojourn in Germany, in the same year Le Corbusier's design for the Ministry of Light Industry building in Moscow began to materialize and Soviet architecture began to win international acclaim. At the same time new groups were formed, such as ''October'' (1928–32), led by two of the Vesnin brothers, V. A. (1882–1950) and A. A. (1883–1959), with its emphasis on polygraphy, photography and poster art. Abstract exhibitions were still tolerated—for instance, the 1929 personal show of Malevich at the Tretyakov Gallery. It was obvious that if art was to become an effective political weapon, then some kind of centralization of artistic energies was needed and the Party itself should take control of the cultural administration.

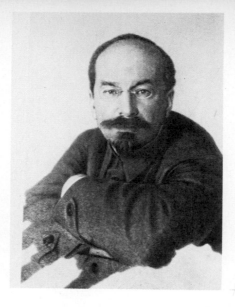

*A. V. Lunacharsky, as a
dramatist and poet and
—chiefly—as the Commissar
for Enlightenment of
"Narkompros," dispensed
great power and influence
among the early leftists.
Photo was taken about 1922.*

*Photographed in 1931—
he was then 53—this is
Kasimir Malevich whose
totally geometric
abstractions based on
Cubism carry the
identifying label that
he himself coined,
"Suprematism." He died
in Leningrad in 1935.*

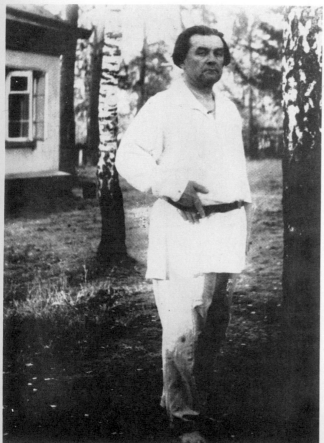

The artist finally lost his independence after the stern measures of the early 1930s. The famous decree of 1932, "On the Reconstruction of Literary and Art Organizations," liquidated all existing art groups and proposed a single union of Soviet artists with a Communist faction therein—in order to overcome "insular reticence" and "alienation from the political tasks of contemporaneity."[23] Two years later, at the First All-Union Conference of Soviet Writers, the principles of Socialist Realism were advocated, echoing Stalin's earlier demand for an art that was "national in form and Socialist in content."[24] With the intrusion of the Party into cultural life, many leftist artists were relieved of their administrative posts and direct contact was established between the political machine and artistic output. As early as 1929 Lunacharsky had resigned as head of Narkompros and had been replaced by the more conservative A. S. Bubnov (1883–1940)—a change which immediately affected the standing of artists: for instance, it had been thanks to Lunacharsky that so many leftists had been given visas to travel abroad, and this privilege was now curtailed. In any case, the leftist ranks were seriously depleted by the late 1920s because of emigration, although Malevich and Tatlin never deserted the new society. Despite inordinate political pressure, in fact, a few courageous artists continued to work as their private beliefs dictated, as far as this was possible. From the late '20s until his death Malevich produced interesting portraits which incorporated the schematicism of Suprematism; in 1933 Tatlin exhibited his designs for his Letatlin flying machine and then continued to experiment in theater decor and easel painting; P. N. Filonov (1883–1941) continued to produce his Expressionistic canvases until his death.

Apart from these isolated figures, the early 1930s can be seen as the period when the last vestiges of artistic extremism gave way to the dictatorship of a political bureaucracy. Even so, it is tempting to conclude that the resultant artistic discipline of Socialist Realism which the Party provided was a bitter, but essential, remedy for the fragmentation confronting leftist art:

at last a cohesive style, a definite school of Soviet painting, was created.

Sources are in Russian, unless otherwise stated.

1. The artist Lentulov maintained that this was the derivation of the name. For Larionov's version, see V. Parkin, "The Donkey's Tail and Target" in the miscellany *The Donkey's Tail and Target* (Moscow: Myunster, 1913).

2. For example, very few of Goncharova's post-1908 works had been purchased, according to the catalogue of her large one-man show in Moscow, 1913.

3. K. S. Malevich, *On New Systems in Art* (Vitebsk, 1919), p. 10. For similar statements see El Lissitzky, "New Russian Art" in *El Lissitzky* by S. Lissitzky-Küppers (New York: New York Graphic Society, 1968), p. 331 (in English), and V. Tatlin, "The Task Ahead of Us" in *Daily Bulletin of the 8th Congress of Councils*, Jan. 1, No. 13 (Moscow, 1921), p. 11.

4. See V. Lenin, *Party Organization and Party Literature*, 1905. In *Lenin—Works* (Moscow-Leningrad, 1929), Vol. 8, pp. 368–90.

5. *Central Committee News*, Dec. 13, No. 250 (Petrograd, 1917), p. 6.

6. A. Efros, "Art and Revolution" in the almanac *Ends without Beginnings*, No. 1 (Moscow, 1922), p. 113. The "Wanderers" were a group of Realist artists who established a series of mobile or "wandering" exhibitions from 1871 until the early 1920s. The Union of Russian Artists, a moderate exhibition society, existed 1903 to 1923.

7. K. Malevich, "Our Tasks" in *Visual Art*, No. 1 (Petrograd, 1919), p. 29.

8. Declaration of Komfut (Communist Futurism) in *Art of the Commune*, Jan. 26, No. 8 (Petrograd, 1919).

9. Part of a poem by V. Kirillov. Quoted from A. Mikhailov, "Lenin and the Struggle with Proletkult and Futurist Distortions [1919–20]" in *Art*, No. 9 (Moscow, 1970), p. 36.

10. Open letter from the Central Committee in *Pravda*, Dec. 1, 1920.

11. V. Lenin, *Lenin on Culture and Art* (Moscow, 1956), p. 250.

12. The original list of "revolutionaries" included such unexpected names as Beethoven, Lermontov and Scriabin as well as the obvious choices of Marx, Engels, etc.

13. *Evening News of the Moscow Council of Workers and Red Army Deputies*, Feb. 10, 1920. The statue was, in fact, demolished.

14. M. Chagall, *My Life* (New York: Orion Press, 1960), p. 139 (in English).

15. Obmokhu was the abbreviation of the Society of Young Artists; it existed as an exhibition group in Moscow from 1919 until 1922.

16. Review of Obmokhu exhibition by V. Solovyev in *Communist Labor* (Moscow), Nov. 17, 1920.

17. At the end of 1926 Vkhutemas was renamed Vkhutein (abbreviation of Higher State Art-Technical Studios). In 1930 this was changed to the Moscow Art Institute.

18. In 1919 Malevich replaced Chagall as head of the school and renamed it Unovis (abbreviation of Affirmation of the New in Art).

19. A. Rylov, *Recollections* (Leningrad, 1960), chapter 51, p. 185.

20. See "Amongst Artists" in *Communist Labor* (Moscow), Nov. 27, 1920. It should be noted that at the same time Lenin paid an official visit to the Moscow Svomas and was disheartened at the predominance of Futurism.

21. In 1928 AKhRR was renamed AKhR (abbreviation of Association of Artists of the Revolution).

22. Preface to catalogue of first exhibition of NOZh, Moscow, November 1922.

23. Text of decree in *On the Party and Soviet Press: A Collection of Documents* (Moscow, 1954), p. 431.

24. J. Stalin, *Collected Works*, 13 vols., Vol. 12 (Moscow, 1951), p. 369.

Art
and the
mass
audience ERNEST VAN DEN HAAG

"The most prominent of the snobberies—
democratic snobbery—seems to
imply that only what attracts great
masses is good, and conversely, what is
good does attract great masses, and
finally, if it does not seem to, it must
have been insufficiently advertised."

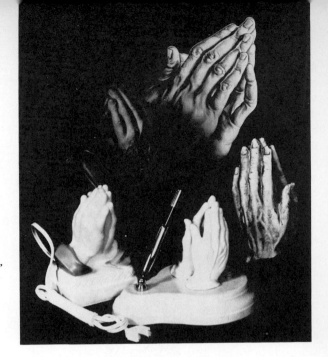

These three-dimensional kitsch interpretations of an Albrecht Dürer drawing, Hands of an Apostle, *reveal one aspect of "a widely shared or mass taste . . . catered to by the production of standardized objects."*

Museums—public collections dedicated to preserving, researching, exhibiting and occasionally cultivating what they collect—are modern institutions responding to modern needs. They are not altogether new. The library at Alexandria might be regarded as a museum (or, as well, a university). And, collecting, of course, has been done since ancient times. Unlike the Greeks, the Romans were collectors: collecting often takes the place of creating, and some of it may well stem from an unconscious recognition of inability to create.

The borderline between some collections and some museums is certainly blurred. Yet, if history is continuous, historiography requires distinctions which, though they may overstress discontinuities, are necessary for analysis: they enable us to perceive differences and changes. With these qualifications I would assert that the modern museum became possible, necessary and useful only as a result of the industrial revolution, which both created and limited the function of museums.

When, about two hundred years ago, men bent their gaze from the heavens to this earth and decided to concentrate on comfort and convenience in their temporal and material life rather than placing all their bets on glory to come, they increased the productivity of their labor for this purpose. They have continued to do so ever since. But they did more. They also created mass production: the efficient production of standardized things by standardized methods; and, of course, mass consumption: widespread demand for the newly produced standardized things. A widely shared or mass taste (or set of mass tastes) had to be created which could be catered to by the production of standardized objects.

People's attitudes toward their work and their life changed. Economic aspirations spread, as did mobility, education, income and highly homogenized tastes and styles, which in turn were mass-produced by such processes as mass education, mass communication, advertising, etc. Since people worked less—fewer hours per day, fewer days per week, fewer weeks per lifetime— time began to hang heavily on their hands. But they earned more too, and numerous products became available to help them kill time—newspapers, movies, TV, mass travel, to name a few. Ultimately there occurred a shift of economic, political and—most important here—cultural power from "the classes" to "the masses." The masses now set the cultural styles. Not that they are not led—they always are. But it is the *masses* that are led (and, therefore, have at least veto power), not a small elite. Whereas profitable production of goods and services in the past largely catered to the rich—whether one has in mind the services of politicians, merchants or artists—now much of it caters to broad masses of consumers. Their purchasing power is incomparably more important than that of the rich. (Even Tiffany's sells to the masses, though partly it sells the snob appeal derived from being reputed to sell to the rich.) It is the masses who create bestsellers, go to the movies, view TV, buy records and make up the vast market for art reproductions. They are beginning even to influence the collectors' market for old and for modern art. These changes have defined, limited and institutionalized the modern museum and now threaten to pervert it.

In former times, art was created for customers who commissioned it: for princes and institutions—the church

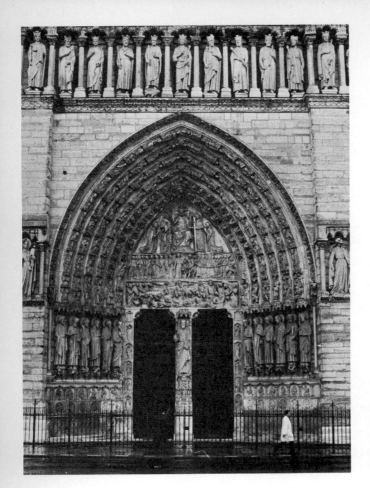

*Principal entrance to the
cathedral of Notre Dame
in Paris. "Art was
usually commissioned for
a specific occasion and
destined to adorn a
specific room, building,
piazza, church, grave, etc."*

being perhaps foremost—or later, for rich merchants
and merchant princes. Thus created, art often was meant
to have specific functions, religious or political, or it
served status maintenance in the tradition of *noblesse
oblige*. In any event, art was usually commissioned for
a specific occasion and destined to adorn a specific room,
building, piazza, church, grave, etc. Often there was
a quite intimate mutual relation between the artist and
the customer. Finally, art was a public matter and a
public issue. Donatello's statues led to near riots in
Florence, and so still did the Fauves centuries later
in Paris. Today, tolerance extends further; or is it indifference? When there is a fuss about a museum's exhibit—as there was about the Metropolitan's "Harlem

on My Mind"—it is never about the esthetic, it is about the political implications.

Isabella d'Este wrote fifty-four letters to Perugino (at least that many remain) about a simple painting she had commissioned. She and the artists lived in the same community in which art mattered. Mantegna's art did well with her fussiness, as did Titian's with that of her brother Alfonso. And the relationship of Michelangelo to Giulio de Medici (Clement VII)—the endless fussy bickering and replanning—is well known. Michelangelo liked it—or so he explained to his pupil Condivi. Today such a participatory relationship is unlikely; the expectation of it would be resented as patron's arrogance and would not be approved by the general public. We assume the patron doesn't understand beans about what the artist is doing (the assumption is often correct) and should, at most, be allowed to buy the stuff as an investment. There is no community, therefore no common language, no communication or common concern (mutual concern is not common concern) and aspiration. One uses the other—politely. Art is no longer part and expression of life, but a special and separate domain of the artist, a domain which should be worshipped and supported by his public, but not actually participated in. (The theatrical arts seem, on the contrary, to try to "involve" the spectator and make him a participant. But not actually so. He is used as a prop rather, and assigned a role. He is not an independent participant—you'd be dead if you acted alive in the Living Theatre. Yet the fumbling attempt indicates a vague perception of something wrong.)

The artist still addresses—or thinks he addresses—the public. But there is no dialogue. He lectures to a mass meeting. Participation has been replaced by indifference, disguised as respect, which inhibits even such hostile participation as marked the reaction of the French bourgeois to the Impressionists.

To be sure, private collectors still are around. Indeed, art collecting has become not only an investment for prestige and status—it always was that, although in a less impersonal way—but also for money. Yet the position of art and artists has changed. In the Middle Ages they were part of the social structure, as craftsmen were. In the Renaissance they moved nearer the center, becoming indispensable to the glory of their patrons. The industrial revolution pushed them away from the center toward the margin. Artists became marginal, dispensable and thereupon obtained the license of fools—they were allowed to lead *la vie de bohème* as Murger imagined it.

After the industrial revolution art no longer was part of the essence of life, nor meant to reveal it. It was treated as decoration, fashion and entertainment. Little public place was left for art—few princely and ecclesiastical commissions, few palaces, churches, public buildings, parks and occasions to celebrate. And little remained of which art could be an emblem and monument. It is hard to celebrate comfort and convenience—though it is not hard to deride it, as Pop art demonstrates. Museums became shelters for art of the past.

Art became homeless—a commodity, not a personal relationship, and alienated from the surrounding reality. This development was intensified as more and more art lost its original home and its original function. Museums not only became shelters, but also—as was said disparagingly—cemeteries of art. Museums cannot be cultivated gardens, let alone natural habitats of living plants. They are places where art is preserved, as dried flowers are. This development surely was not the fault or the doing of the museums. The function of graveyards was forced on them; someone had to give a decent burial to art, a sepulcher had to be found so that the unburied bodies would not be lying around, a nuisance, and also a burden on people's consciences when the works were gnawed at by commercial rodents. Now, as Ugo Foscolo so lyrically wrote in his great poem *Dei Sepolchri,* cemeteries are monuments to the affection borne by survivors to their dead, to the continuity of human civilization, and of its institutions. Ancestral graves may inspire deeds, may broaden and deepen our experience of life, and may help us to develop what

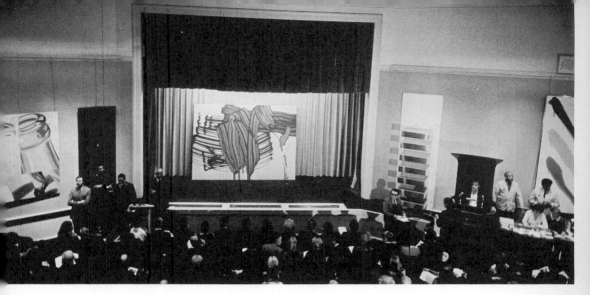

our ancestors started, or to continue it. And, this too is the function of museums.

Surely in fulfilling all these functions—in preserving art, making it available to scholars and artists, displaying it to the public, in rescuing the artistic past from destruction and oblivion—museums have their hands full. Or so one might think. But it seems that all this does not keep them, or their ambitious directors, busy enough. They feel left out. They are not satisfied with being curators of cemeteries, however marvelous the illustrious remains, however great the monuments in their care. They do not want power over the dead. They want power among the living. To fulfill this ambition they do three things.

First, they become acquisitive. Additional purchases steadily add to collections. Never mind that there is not enough space to display what is already there. More can be built. If I can add to collections and buildings, I have made, out of this monument to the past, a monument to my living self as well. And, while doing so, I must be reckoned a force on art markets, and among artists, builders, politicians, donors, collectors. I will preside not over a cemetery, but over a growing empire. So used, the past will give me power, and increase my present status. (Of course, to make occasional well-selected acquisitions is among the tasks of the museum

At a Parke-Bernet auction sale on Nov. 18, 1970, left to right: Silver Skies *by James Rosenquist (1962), sold for $27,500; Roy Lichtenstein's* Big Painting No. 6 *(1965), sold for $75,000; and Don Judd's* Unit Modular Sculpture *(1967), sold for $8,500. "Art collecting has become not only an investment for prestige and status . . . but also for money."*

director. But this task is as easily distinguished from what has just been described as normal nourishment is from greedy overeating and the consequent obesity.)

Second, these additional purchases then are used to attract great masses to the museums. Look, we don't only have the Rembrandts you are bored by. We also have a new Rembrandt! Which must be wonderful! It cost a million! Look at it! It is new! new! new! And so they troop in, lured not by interest in art, or the past, but by interest in the sensational, the new, the expensively prestigious. A similar motivation underlies not a few—though by no means all—special exhibits.

The ambitious museum director may also resort to making his museum a cultural conglomerate. Thus he may put on exhibitions of photographs about the life (not the art, the life) of a fashionable minority group— anything to get people involved, to lure people not interested in art into the museum. It is the number that counts, not what they are doing there, nor what leads them there or what they gain by coming there. Never mind, then, that these people attracted *ad majorem directoris gloriam* may disturb those who actually want to see the things the museum was to cultivate. There are more people who care little and understand less of art than there are people who care and understand. Hence the former matter more. After all, the more people the museum becomes important to, the more people its director becomes important to, and the more important he feels. We live in an age of mass production and consumption. Even snobbery is sustained by the number of people one is known to, rather than by their quality.

Now, it is true that many people go to a museum out of mixed motives, and snobbery frequently plays a part in the enjoyment of its treasures. I am not against snobbery—the wish to be associated with one's betters, or those of higher status, to be counted among them— even though this, almost by definition, confuses appearance and reality. However, I am against deliberately catering to it in the place of cultivating art. It is true that most people do not see paintings so much as themselves looking at the paintings. They do not really see what the painter painted, but rather his reputation, his brand name, as it were. If the painting were replaced by mediocre imitations, they might admire them as easily as the originals—until told. (Perhaps, then, they are gazing at least as much at the reputation of the painting as at the painting.) Still, this kind of snobbery seems preferable to that of people—and of administrators who cater to them—who come to look at exhibits as though they were celebrities, because they are in the news. Directors who themselves want to be in the news get there by "making news," buying or doing things that are "newsworthy." They themselves become celebrities and are looked in on by those who look at whatever is in the news.

There is a confluence of several forms of snobbery here. They have in common only that they all endanger the actual mission of the museum. The most prominent of the snobberies—democratic snobbery—seems to imply that only what attracts great masses is good, and conversely, what is good does attract great masses, and finally, if it does not seem to, it must have been insufficiently advertised. A corollary is that any means, even the most dubious, if they succeed in attracting great masses, can be used, for "success" justifies. The masses cannot but benefit from their presence in the museum, whatever brought them there. No matter that the people attracted may neither learn anything nor enjoy any of the works of art at the museum. It's the body count that matters. It is assumed—by definition, not evidence—that anyone who comes goes away improved. (Art is thought of as an instrument of improvement—an effect it has neither on those who care for it nor on those who come and don't.) Hence one must lure people to museums by any kind of gimmick, for it is good *per se* to attract more people to museums at whatever cost to the museum function, and, one is tempted to add, to the memory of the dead muses.

A third way of perverting the museum's function is to collect contemporary art. Some museums are dedicated to nothing less. They are honest. But they should not have to exist. What artists now create ought to be created for an understanding public, for persons or public institutions interested in buying what they create. If there are no such persons I doubt that artists can create any art. A museum seems as unlikely to replace purchasers as a cemetery is to replace life. One hardly encourages a mother by telling her she bears children so that they may be decently buried. In the end, indeed. But there is life between birth and death. And so with works of art. If any are to be created, they cannot be created for museums. Nor can museums—possibly their final resting place—replace the life that works of art, if they are to be alive, must be created for.

If one leaves the metaphor of the cemetery, it still remains an unavoidable fact that nobody lives in a museum. One goes specifically to see the exhibits, one next to the other. But how can a work of art live under these circumstances? No more than a person who spends his life bereft of a personal environment, a habitat to which he relates and which becomes, or was created as, an extension of his personality.

This is not to deny that the purchase (and exhibition) of contemporary art by museums helps contemporary artists; it may even be the best that can be done. Such purchases also document our times for future historians and anthropologists. Nonetheless, to make of museums not the last resting place of works of art but their immediate destination is to avow that works of art have no function in our society and no place to go. Under these circumstances I cannot see how they can be created.

Along a New Jersey highway, motorists who otherwise might never see the masterpiece are regaled by the famed Blue Boy. "Art is thought of as an instrument of improvement —an effect it has neither on those who care for it nor on those who don't."

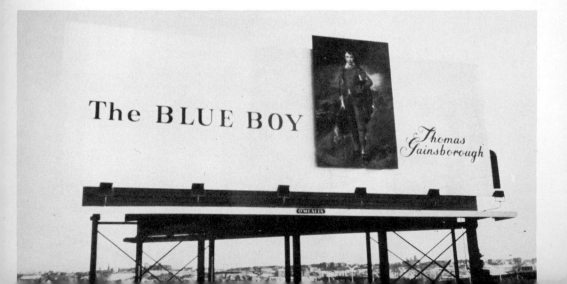

The museum and the democratic fallacy

BRYAN ROBERTSON

". . . the public, conditioned by the strenuous and massively simple slogans of advertising and the super-realistic giantism of cinemascope, now expects to find a commensurate spectacle at the museum and is dismayed not to find some semblance of showbiz glitter in the permanent collections as well as temporary installations. But it is absurd that the *size* of an audience should take precedence over *what happens* to visitors inside a museum. Numbers may relate to a democracy but not to art."

Very few people can read. The general level of illiteracy is rising fast. Retaining information from the printed page with any degree of precision has always been a hit-or-miss affair anyway, since those who can read mostly do so with willful selectivity, extracting whatever suits a personal taste, need or prejudice rather than the exact substance of a written account. A rather different kind of visual capriciousness is in action when works of art are looked at in museums, but both share failings peculiar to our era: an inability to concentrate and a lack of time—or, more tellingly, inclination—to pay prolonged and patient attention to what is in front of the viewer.

The museum-going public, like any other, is subject to certain forms of conditioning, to particular disabilities, that are common to the present. Among them is the decline in power of the printed word with the exactitude of its authority as a reference, and the ascendancy of those branches of the mass media which register a more atmospheric impression of events, ideas and opinions. Even newspapers have been affected through competition by the visual impact of TV: observable in their increase of pictorial coverage as well as features, compartmenting and layout. Most people are content to be fed aurally by radio, with sound employed like Musak whether it is music or the spoken word, or visually by films and TV, with images reinforced by sound. Both are of an excessively simplified character so as to be as nonabrasive as possible to the generally relaxed awareness. If something is underlined to claim more than a flicker of response, it is accentuated in a comfortably predictable way. "Presentation" is devouring all the arts: it is now even prized above content in many of them. In the mass media which have stimulated this attitude, and to which the museum public is certainly exposed for information or entertainment (the two are merging into one), presentation has already degenerated into systematic processing. There is a danger that museums are being affected by this retrogression, for which large attendance figures can supply no alibi but only compound the fault.

It would be agreeable to suppose that the abandonment of reading and the loss of literature were giving place, through a more widespread use of imagery, to a revivified extension of the visual faculty. But this is not so because the mass media reduce everything to a point of insistent triviality. The supposedly more rarefied or thoughtful imagery, some might say "abstract" imagery, of avant-garde film might seem to oppose this: but essentially even the best filmmakers think in terms of pictorial journalism. The work of Jean-Luc Godard and others could not exist in terms of speed, cutting and stylistic bias without the example of commercial TV. Filmmakers are not alone, of course, in absorbing visual treatment, consciously or otherwise, from commercial art. Pop art is a final extraction. Visual style was once sifted down from higher forms of art to lower echelons which borrowed and adapted it. Now it is dredged up, without any compensatory transformation, from commonplace levels where its marginal function is to invest a slackened style, derived from higher sources, with a spurious vitality remote from its initial imaginative energy. Trivialization has many guises.

We subsist in our daily lives on a flow of imagery and sound that is mainly inflated, distorted or coarsened. The public is almost conditioned to a state of unquestioning visual illiteracy to match the lack of aural selectivity already established through increasing tolerance to haphazard noise. Spectacles are now listed under "cosmetics."

Indiscriminate visual or perceptual infantilism, together with a lack of aural sensitivity, prevails for the overwhelming majority of people who are already illiterate as readers through sparse education, or because the activity of reading has been undermined by the assault of easier and swifter alternatives. This is grimly paradoxical at a time when, we are told, instant and elaborate communication is available for everyone. There is very little communication in depth, and the prospect holds scant hope for optimism: violence and misery are not the only kinds of imagery to be already emotionally nullified through a literal process of degradation. Eventually, a mindless vacuum could be attained, undisturbed by the slightest emotional, intel-

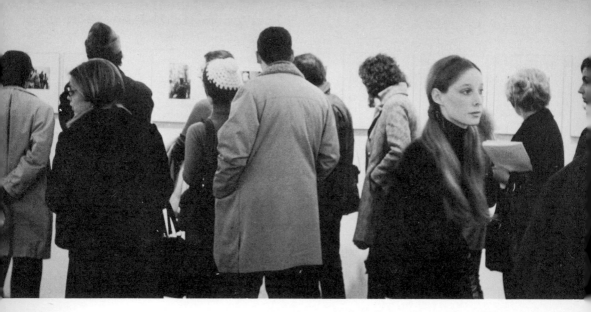

Any city, any museum, any peak hour for crowds— ". . . visiting museums is an unconscious form of freely associative but hopeful ancestor worship by a dispossessed tribe that has also lost its historical records, or never knew them."

lectual or retinal challenge but confirmed from time to time by the reassurance of nostalgic clichés.

Meanwhile, a vast public surges through our museums which might be reached, with care, if due consideration were given to its precarious reflexes and blunted, confused sensibility. The trouble here is that this public has never been sufficiently analyzed: large attendance statistics suffice as evidence, for most museum directors, of enthusiastic public involvement. But attendance can exist at many levels, not all of them significant. There is no doubt that, for a substantial majority, visiting a museum is a more communal extension of watching TV, a means of passing the time, a form of passive entertainment that was usually free until recently and is still comparatively cheap. There is nothing wrong with this: some proportion of visitors intent upon relaxation may come away with new imaginative insights gained involuntarily and by chance; in any case there is a place for relaxation which museums can certainly occupy, coincidentally with their other functions, as well as continuing to provide a convenient meeting place or a refuge from bad weather. For another large section of the public, rather more active in its response, visiting museums is an unconscious form of freely associative but hopeful ancestor worship by a dispossessed tribe that has also lost its historical records, or never knew them. The more conscious spearhead of this section is formed by those for whom art is a possible substitute for religious impulses, frustrated by an age of disbelief. There is the inevitable search for identity, the desire for cultural prestige, the development of social snobbery, and fashion.

None of this matters; for beyond all these factors there is always the reassurance provided by a number of visitors to museums who may be there in the straightforward hope of enlightenment. And it is here that the more subtle aspects of present-day confusion need attention. Because there is a search for enlightenment, it does not necessarily follow that enlightenment will come from works of art. Only an exceedingly small proportion of those who enter a museum are even remotely prepared for what awaits them, and only a total revolution in our educational system could remedy this deficiency. It would then take at least a decade for the results of this revolution to be felt. Anyone interested in an analysis of such a revolution should read Herbert Read's *Education through Art,* one of the few great books on art and in this case a unique one. But our existing system of education is a direct reflection of the structure and values retained by our society, and there would have to be a profound social revolution before Read's educational principles could be established. And if education reflects society it should be remembered that ours is predominantly a producer-consumer society, and art is therefore taught in our schools from a producer-consumer point of view: both in theory and by application. Art is there; it exists; therefore it can be bought or acquired or absorbed. It is not as simple as that. Much of the art practiced today is, in its shallowness, the direct consequence of the producer-consumer orientation, and it is experienced and assessed from much the same viewpoint. When this viewpoint is still further undermined by the trivialized perception and mental processing of a public created by mass media, false values are inevitable.

There is, too, the simplistic notion that because we live in a democracy, and museums exist for everybody, everybody must not only respond to art but like it. You can certainly teach the rudiments of visual education, and if Read's theory of education through art were realized there is no doubt that the world would be a better place and, as an agreeable bonus, everyone would be more visually conscious; but real visual perception in depth has always been, and would remain, a rarity. For this involves all of our faculties and more knowledge, more concentration, more imagination than most of us possess. There are critics who can record shifts in style; like performing seals, collectors can then jump through the appropriate hoops. Given the development of art since the Renaissance, a true understanding of what makes a masterpiece (which practically never fits into a producer-consumer pattern and cannot easily be absorbed by any society) is possible only for a minority, however, and it is this recognition alone that is of crucial, life or death consequence. Useless to say that masterpieces are inappropriate for our time, because everyone is looking for one—whilst society in a producer-consumer democracy makes their creation almost an impossibility.

Many people can never be fully responsive visually: their kind of brain, their sensory equipment, however educated, does not travel instinctively toward visual stimulus. Why is a scientist not a sculptor? In the arts, some people respond to poetry or to literature, others to music, others to painting. Some are happy with all three, but not everybody is going to be at his best when confronted by visual art. You can be tone-deaf but still be an extremely sensitive individual; there is no disgrace in a lack of dominant visual receptivity. Nor is there anything to complain about in the idea of a "minority." Because some minorities have been oppressed, the word has taken on a reprehensible connotation, but it should be remembered, also, that most human progress has been achieved by minorities throughout history— and that Stravinsky, for example, was a minority of one. Creative, or at least constructive, minorities should be encouraged; all you can do, in a democracy, is to make it possible for a minority to expand. The alternative to an "elite," if this is the word that must now be employed, is the prevalence of mediocrity. But in fact the avoidance, let alone the suppression, of an elite is impossible. Only snobbery, inverse or otherwise, is bothered by the idea of an elite. Or, in a totalitarian state, fear of an elite's knowledge and insight.

Democratic thinking about art and a potential audience also forgets that the confrontation between the general public and great historical art, let alone the serious art of its own time, is a comparatively recent phenomenon: as recent as public museums with free or cheap admittance. How many people entering a museum know that the word itself means "temple of the muses," first built by Ptolemy, Alexander's lieutenant, at Alexandria, where performances of music, dance and poetry took place at a site adjoining the first great library and collection of antiquities? For most people, the word museum is synonymous with mausoleum; some kind of consecration of the especially gifted dead is sensed. More practically, the building is thought of as a depository for loot. The example of Napoleon's plunder from the Nile, housed at the requisitioned Palais du Louvre, probably accounts for the modern confusion.

The comparative newness of this confrontation between the general public and serious art is usually overlooked. But to go back only a short way, in the eighteenth century there were prints for popular consumption, technically brilliant and esthetically sanctified by the talents and the fame of the artist who either made them or authorized their production; there were also popular prints made specially for a wide audience by satirists like Hogarth, Gillray and many others: "penny plain, tuppence coloured." There was also folk art of all kinds which persisted until the close of the nineteenth century, that same century which saw the advent of beautifully illustrated books by "Phiz," Dicky Doyle, Tenniel and others; and then there were brilliantly inventive posters—but who is the twentieth-century Lautrec? Mass media will support a style, suitably processed, but not an inspired painter-draftsman as an individual force.

And Lautrec was the graphic poet for unique occasions, not bulk merchandizing. The public has been deprived of popular art in the twentieth century and is left with a hunger for which the stylistic sophistication of Raymond Loewy or Saul Bass is no answer.

Pop art, whatever its merits or faults, is impelled as much by the angry nihilism of Céline as it is by affectionate taxidermy or the colder exploitation, satirical or formal, of the manic world of comic strips. None of these motives, so clear in the work, inspires popular trust; in any case, pop art is sealed off in museums or acquired by wealthy collectors with a special taste. Its heyday marked a further extension of the expropriation and erosion of the ''Left Bank'' by the ''Right Bank,'' beginning when Buffet's gaunt and anguished Existentialist lovers (in themselves trivialized) or equally emaciated and frugal interiors were bought, in bright gold frames, by rich industrialists who wanted a safe whiff of Montparnasse. The same gilded emasculation can be seen at work in the proliferation of expensive restaurants which affect the atmosphere of scruffy bistros. Supposedly democratic, the entire drift is similar to the condescension shown by society women, internationally in the twenties, who thought it amusing and exciting to go around with miners in cloth caps or black or white prizefighters.

There is also the virtual disappearance from public view of any vestige of ornament. It is banished from our Bauhaus-derived buildings, and from any integral or instinctive part of our interiors. Handbooks of ornament will parade elaborately through its entire history in diagrammatic form, but stop blankly at the turn of the century. Ornament has gone; and its suppression has left an habitual appetite unsatisfied except through constant revivalism and its reappearance, disguised with much intellectual and esthetic pretentiousness, as several (though not all) forms of abstract painting. Abstract art is the visual language of our time and has reached stirring climaxes; but a good deal of abstract painting now is an attempt to provide collectors and a public starved of ornament with a new form of decoration *in vacuo* and, obliquely, to provide the modern equivalents of the similarly proscribed non-utilitarian *objet de luxe.*

Deprived of its own popular art, faced by the demise of folk art, robbed of nonfunctional decoration or ornament and denied nonutilitarian luxury, the public will certainly rush into museums—but without much awareness of its urgent reasons. Given educational limitations, the general pressures against sustained thought or concentration, and the bludgeoning of sensory apparatus by mass media, noise and "presentation" that has evolved into systematic processing, it should be apparent that unless the contents of a museum are merely to lapse into yet another aspect of distanced unreality, the institution must consider its public with immense care and understanding. There is evidence, on the contrary, that museums are possibly extending the harm already done, through shallow thinking and methods sustained by the unquestioning acceptance of high attendance figures.

The need has never been greater for rigorous standards and their most scrupulous observance. But museums seem increasingly anxious to race the dealers in their

Lobby, the Seagram building, New York. ". . . the virtual disappearance from public view of any vestige of ornament. It is banished from our Bauhaus-derived buildings, and from any integral or instinctive part of our interiors. . . . Ornament has gone; and its suppression has left an habitual appetite unsatisfied." Photo, © Ezra Stoller (ESTO).

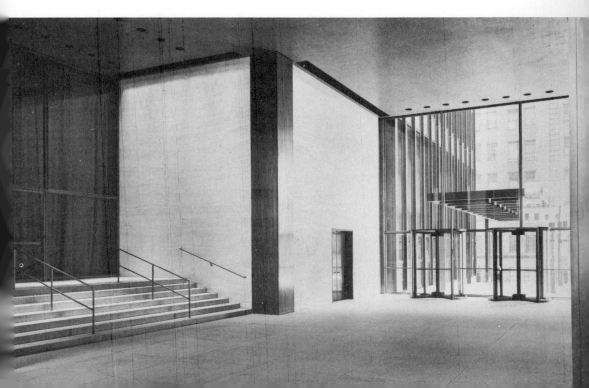

efforts to promote new art (though a high proportion of it is temporary and provisional in its lack of spiritual weight, not unlike the banners and devices once carried aloft by crowds in processions, centuries ago) and have not yet solved the problem of serving scholarship as well as the needs of an uninformed public in their attempts to house old art. The first charge is easily answered: promotion is a commercial activity best left to merchants. But in that very answer is the key to the second impasse. Museums have collections of many kinds of objects as well as paintings. These collections, in their various groups, are of uneven esthetic value. At one time, collections were kept intact because for a serious student the unevenness in itself is instructive: the flaws and failures of design, the repetition and the eccentricities of form among a collection of Benin bronzes, for example, can convey much of the values, traditions and derivations of the society which produced the bronzes as well as the peaks and splendors, weaknesses and limitations of their artistic capability. Increasingly, however, in recent years, the integrity of these collections has been broken by museum personnel concerned with display: the one treasure has been extracted, placed alone in a case and tactfully lit against a tasteful background, and the rest of the collection banished to the cellars where scholars who know of its existence can explore it separately. This act of censorship through isolation is undertaken on behalf of the general public, and it certainly makes museums easier places to visit for the majority. But presentation of this kind, now *de rigueur,* entails more than one step toward falsification.

There is a story of the late Queen Mary visiting the newly refurbished and reorganized Victoria and Albert Museum in London, shortly after the war. A fusty and crowded interior had been transformed beautifully by a director with taste and an awareness of the new role museums were to play with the public. The royal visitor was knowledgeable and made a serious tour of the museum: a single priceless Sung bowl was in one subtly lit case, one great example of medieval embroidery in another, and so on. When the tour was concluded, Queen Mary congratulated the director on the new interior, thanked him, and then said as she left: "But what a pity everything looks as if it's for sale." The producer-consumer era in museums had begun.

It is not easy for museums, eager to please a large public, to avoid betrayal of the works of art and the values entrusted to them, or to confuse that trust in other ways by housing unworthy objects. The public expects to find authoritative standards of excellence and is certainly confused by work which more properly belongs to an experimental arts laboratory or to the pages of an *engagé* art journal. At the same time, museums face acute problems through the way in which the public, conditioned by the strenuous and massively simple slogans of advertising and the super-realistic giantism of cinemascope, now expects to find a commensurate spectacle at the museum and is dismayed not to find some semblance of showbiz glitter in the permanent collections as well as temporary installations. But it is absurd that the *size* of an audience should take precedence over *what happens* to visitors inside a museum. Numbers may relate to a democracy but not to art.

Curators and exhibition planners walk a curious tightrope: a public used to the brilliance of theatrical lighting does not, for example, understand the purity of effect transmitted by a large show of Rothko, or Morris Louis, whose color-saturated canvases are diminished and not enhanced by artificial illumination, however subtle, and can only "breathe" properly and exude their proper glow in plain daylight or the softest and most muted, indirect, artificial lighting. If these conditions are honored, the public feels that the exhibition is only half alive: *the lights* are missing. These reactions were noted in London some years back in a large public gallery filled with daylight, in early summer. In New York recently, at a spectacular exhibition including many masterpieces, an attempt was made to make things easier for the public which involved the wrong kind of concentration: a number of small sculptures were placed on a revolving stand in a spotlit glass case. Apart from the Ziegfeld and Busby Berkeley influence, the effect was trivializing to art and completely opposed the basic principle that sculpture is essentially static with movement implied *within* that static condition: it is the spectator who is supposed to move and put a little thought and work into heights and angles of vision, not kinetic presentation.

But if the gentle corruptions demanded in wooing the public can achieve their own distortions, which the museums should resist, there are others that strike deeper at the roots of artistic truth. If art is not a commodity to be "sold," it is not just information either; and a great work of art has nothing to do with communication in its immediately effective and popular sense. Communication is for the telephone or cable, for speech or for writing: there are less laborious ways of "communicating" than by painting a picture or constructing a sculpture. A great painting or sculpture detonates forces in our imagination which transform life. Art is concerned with an act of revelation, no less, as immense in inspired implication and mysterious resonance as a Biblical miracle: it comes to us instinct with feeling and must be received with feeling. A great work of art proclaims that two plus two equals five: this truth cannot be rationally communicated, only imaginatively apprehended, and it needs time to grow. A book takes two hours or a week to read, a symphony occupies half an hour of attention; people look at a painting and expect immediate "communication." If these definitions are considered, even the provision of concrete information too near a work of art can swerve or disrupt its potentiality to expand imaginatively in the mind of the spectator, thus diminishing and circumscribing its power. Such power demands tactful intermediaries. The first task of a museum is to give maximum life to a work of art by allowing it to live free of fixed and static lighting, untrammeled by distracting labels and display techniques, and thus to grow in the imagination of visitors. It is lack of imagination which inhibits the true quality of life: the discovery of relativity, or of penicillin, was an act of the imagination more than anything else.

In describing the grim paradox of the illiteracy and visual infantilism of the public at a time of supposedly total communication, one further deadening action should be described. This is the way in which serious issues are continually presented on TV or in magazines— so glamorously and elaborately that the very manner of their coverage implies that the serious issue has been dealt with, solved, disposed of. This is an even more lethal example of the conspicuous waste-disposal system. The confrontation with life must be painless: its exposure must have a built-in bromide. Art can so easily be muffled in this way.

In their eagerness to project more and more art at increasing hordes of people, museums can also reflect the trivialization achieved by TV cultural programs in which presentation, arrived at by a terror of boring the viewers, reduces everything to the same level—Einstein or Bernstein—and we are left with the impression that everything is of equal stature. Similarly, sumptuously mounted exhibitions of masterpieces, in their blaze of showbiz lighting, can lapse into the counterfeit dimension of a coffee-table art book with glossy color plates. But producer-consumer societies involve conspicuous waste, as well as the voracious consumption of style which now demands constant revivals; so perhaps this lavish expendability, this reduction to theatricality, is understandable.

A final irony is that the legitimate channels of communication for the art world, as indeed for any other public, are getting increasingly untrustworthy at the very moment when everyone believes they are receiving total exposure. At the end of 1970, the International Press Institute published a report expressing its profound unease at the widening gap between publishers and their newsrooms. Newspapers of high quality, for instance, publish special supplements covering the economic and social life of a particular country: it is presumed that these supplements are factually correct, but the power of advertisers can substantially slant them one way or another; truth is often suppressed. In the field of art magazines, we are shown only what an idiosyncratic editor believes to be valid: this can be extremely limited in its bearings. Commitment is an honorable estate, but unquestionably it means the promotion of one or two specialized facets of the art scene at the expense of surveys in breadth. Some good art, some-where, invariably falls outside these narrow lines of demarcation and is lost to view. There is also the fact that dealers and others who are willing to pay for ex-pensive color plates secure space in periodicals for certain artists. Promotion, presentation and distortion enter again. Communication in depth, in the normal sense, is far shallower, slower and less reliable than it was in the medieval period when visual and literary style was transmitted by monks wandering across different countries from one monastery to another. Style is now propagated by such superficial means, so often by reproduction, that it is not surprising to find artists barrenly working at format itself, without substance, as a subject. The public finds this hard to comprehend and museums are not helping them.

Apart from unreliability in the traditional forms of communication allowed a democratic public concerned with art, there is the disconcerting truth that while we are living in what is often referred to as a culturally "open situation," without barriers, an implacable force is at work to restrict both the channels of information and the kind of art which might be acceptable among its pace-setters, and therefore suitable for dissemination. First, periodicals everywhere are numerically shrinking. The number of newspapers that can be bought in, say, London or New York, is far smaller than it was a few years ago. Economic and other factors are producing a monolithic structure, as opposed to diversity. This is not unlike the take-over phenomenon in political parties in countries where a broad spectrum was a matter of traditional pride, in favor of a heavily simplified, black-or-white alternative provided by only two parties. Choice is pared down with great intensity; there is an urge toward simplification. Similarly, if we accept that there is now an open situation in art, it is curious to find that the most successful and widely known art is that which suppresses everything in favor of a radically simplified image. Newman and Rothko, for instance, or Noland and Stella, are serious and good artists, but their work concentrates on elimination and divulges something, finally, that is extremely refined and ruthlessly autocratic for a democratic audience.

We are left with the question of a suitable art for a democratic public. It would have to be outside museums: in public buildings, in the streets and squares and parks—and so far it has not arrived. It is doubtful if the public would recognize it if it came, and questionable if it would be popular. It probably exists already as much as it ever will in advertising and street signs and furniture. For great art is safe inside a museum, or relatively harmless; habituation to art through prolonged exposure in everyday life could be dangerous enough to alter society from the deepest level. Herbert Read was a lifelong anarchist, well aware of the anarchy of art and the democratic fallacy when applied to art. The sad thing is that the recent art made by artists for sites far from museums is mainly mannerist and authoritarian; many of the conditions of sadomasochism obtain; and in its determination to be conceptual, an impossible premise for any art, we are faced with art criticism in practice: an interminable and leaden commentary on art rather than art itself. It is curious to find artists of this persuasion in museums again, after apparently rejecting these institutions. They are only too anxious to deposit tons of masonry in one museum, or at least to leave plans and advertisements for their excavations and sites on public display. They are ready to demand that a sixty-foot-long hanging cloth by a colleague be removed from the ceiling of another museum because it spoils the structural sight-lines. The final apotheosis will no doubt amplify the rich folly inherent in the interplay between museums and the democratic fallacy, which museums should perhaps try to redefine. For acting as a willful *deus ex machina* between the two, however thin and impoverished his present clothing, is that unpredictable, anarchic aristocrat, quite lost in a democracy: the artist.

The beleaguered director

THOMAS W. LEAVITT

"He is not really the primary target; he just happens to be in the middle of no-man's-land. Salvation for him, and perhaps for art museums, rests in his ability to resist paranoia and to realize that most of the criticisms directed at him come from extremely limited perspectives. No doubt many of the premises upon which museums were originally founded need drastic revision to maintain contact with contemporary human values. But it is also evident that museums simply cannot provide all things cultural to all people."

Fiske Kimball glowered at us for a long moment in silence. Finally he spoke: "I don't suppose any of these bright young people knows much of anything?" Thus in 1954 the elite Harvard museum class was greeted by the director of the Philadelphia Museum of Art. The question was really rhetorical, but John Coolidge, who with Professor Jakob Rosenberg had guided us patiently through most of the year's work, replied with uncharacteristic meekness that in truth we probably didn't know much yet. How right he was!

Kimball led us through the galleries of the museum, pausing here and there to exclaim about a piece he especially cherished—a Desiderio bas-relief, a dramatic pietà by Rogier van der Weyden, the great Bathers by Cézanne—muttering on one occasion about a recently hired curatorial assistant who knew the exact date of every Picasso but didn't know a Botticelli from a Raphael. Our tour terminated at the cafeteria, where he indicated with a flourish that we peons could buy our own lunches. We were impressed.

But then, we had been impressed in New York by the baroque grandeur of Francis Taylor and the nonchalance of James Rorimer, who told us of a recent gift of $10,000,000 to the Cloisters and then capped it with, "But, really, what can you do with only $10,000,000?" Indeed, all of the museum directors we met that year projected strong personal styles, from the incredibly shy but shrewd George Stout at Worcester to the vibrant Adelyn Breeskin in Baltimore and the elegant David Finley at the National Gallery. We thought of them all as giants.

In 1954 we did not realize that we were near the end of an era in the evolution of museum directors. Even today most of the directors of that time are remembered as being larger than life. The breed which followed these heroic figures was more professional, better educated perhaps, certainly more prosaic. With a few notable exceptions, the grand style was gradually replaced with businesslike attention to growth and service. Most of the great collections had already been wooed and won, and the spirit of the late fifties and early sixties called for consolidation, building expansion, larger education departments, and efforts to entice a wider cross section of the public into museums.

This transition in the general style of museum directors is certainly not the first to have occurred. Perhaps the earliest museum directors were the caretakers of the great European art collections formed in the seventeenth and eighteenth centuries. Often the noble collector himself would act as the director, showing with pardonable pride his acquired treasures. Visitors were almost exclusively aristocrats or artists, and the problem of communication was minimal. Until the French revolution, at least, museum directors had no difficulties with their public.

In the United States the earliest museums were appropriately more popular and commercial in origin. Charles Willson Peale, for example, brought together an amazing array of paintings, sculpture, stuffed animals, fossils and whatever curiosities he could find that might interest and inform the people. His museum, and others like it, flourished in a time when amateurs could appreciate equally the wonders of nature and the work of artists who captured nature on canvas. Other predecessors of modern museums could be found in the galleries of literary clubs like the Boston Athenaeum and artist academies such as the National Academy in New York. In the nineteenth century these galleries displayed almost exclusively the works of living American artists and reflected the close harmony of current taste with the most avant-garde art movements. They were often operated by artists, and there probably has never been a time in which American artists were in closer touch with the public presentation of their work.

The foundation in America of art museums in the modern sense coincides with the rise of great industrial fortunes in the 1860s and 1870s. The Fullers in Boston, Andrew Carnegie in Pittsburgh, J. P. Morgan in New York, bought great (and not so great) old and modern masters in Europe and advocated the formation of major public collections in America, so that Americans would no longer have to feel culturally inferior to the aristocrats of France and England. Modern museums of art in this country thus began with the patronage of

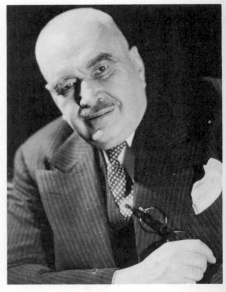

Fiske Kimball, director, Philadelphia Museum of Art, 1925–55.

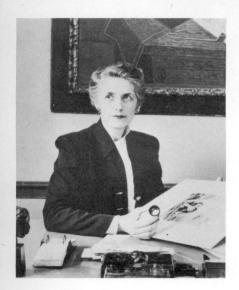

Adelyn Breeskin, director,
Baltimore Museum
of Art, 1947–62.

the wealthy. The directors employed by these wealthy founders reflected their values and like them talked idealistically of art for all the people, all the while presenting priceless treasures with little attention to communication (or scholarship), and building imposing mausoleums which would certainly intimidate any "undesirables." In the first quarter of this century most of the major museums grew even more impressively as the founders and their successors died off, bequeathing collections often of remarkable quality to their favorite institutions.

By the late 1920s and increasingly in the 1930s major collections were already becoming scarce. Art-historical scholarship had advanced to the point where some of the young museum directors really knew quite a bit about the works entrusted to their care and were acutely aware of opportunities for snagging the few remaining important collections. The competition for these collections was stiff; the most successful directors were those who could converse as equals with the moguls of industry, and with their oftentimes more sophisticated daughters and sons, impressing them with their knowledge as well as with the force of their personalities. In those times museum directors were riding high, hobnobbing with the very rich, seldom challenged by scholars, much less by a public which never felt completely at home in the marble palaces erected amid the characteristic ugliness of American cities. It was the tail end of that era that the Harvard museum class of 1954 was witnessing. Within a few years most of the famous directors we had met were gone, some retired, others dead. By the time we really had learned something and had achieved responsible positions, the old élan was largely gone, and we found that we were expected to perform new functions in society.

Above all we were called upon to build. New museums were springing up everywhere, and since the great givers were gone, we had to raise the money with massive drives piloted by professional fund-raising firms. We often were called upon to function as architectural consultants as well as public-relations experts; and many times our lack of experience in those roles created frustrating problems for ourselves and our institutions.

We were also deluged with demands for educational services from a public which was just discovering what "fun" museums could be. As the country-club tone of museums disappeared, private funds became harder to solicit and we had to build cases for public tax support from cities, counties, states and, finally, the federal government. And virtually all of these funds from public sources were conditional upon our performing additional services for the public. These additional services in turn required more staff and facilities and therefore higher expenses and often bigger deficits.

Museum boards of trustees, we found, are predominantly populated by successful businessmen, many of whom see museums as small nonprofit business concerns. In a way, they are, and many techniques of business administration are extremely useful in the operation of museums; but how can you convince a business-oriented trustee that an exhibition of mid-nineteenth-century academic painting is more significant than yet another exhibit of Vincent van Gogh, in spite of the latter's tremendous appeal and esthetic superiority? How can you get an efficiency-minded board to release a top curator for several weeks or months of research that may never even result in an exhibition? By what means can you persuade merchants that an education program that is going great guns ought to be discontinued because its aims and methods are educationally unsound? Undoubtedly it is true that museum directors are sometimes unbusinesslike and inefficient in their conducting of museum affairs, but one cannot be everything, and perhaps there are other qualities . . .

Artists will certainly tell you that there are! As the museum became increasingly public, artists began to realize that, compared to other performers, they had been ruthlessly exploited by the system. Once a work leaves an artist's hands he usually loses all control over it. He has no say in determining the context in which it will be shown, he receives no further royalty or fee from its exhibition, and he has no opportunity to share in

James J. Rorimer, director, Metropolitan Museum of Art, 1955–66. Photo © Karsh, Ottawa.

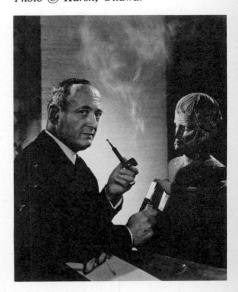

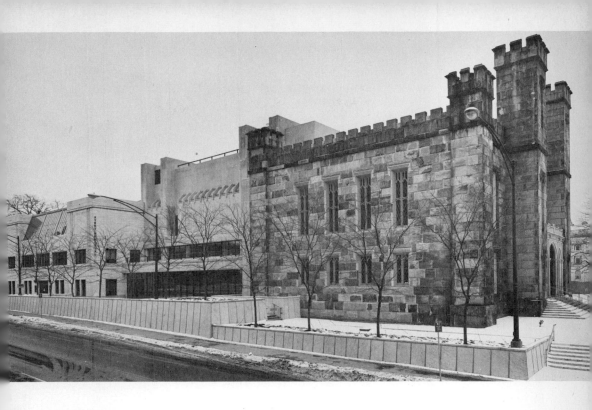

A capsule history of
twentieth-century American
museum architecture—
from traditional through
old-with-new to new.

Left: The City Art Museum,
St. Louis, constructed
for the Louisiana Purchase
Exposition in 1904.
Above: The Wadsworth
Atheneum complex in Hartford,
Connecticut, with the recent
Goodwin Building linking
the Avery Memorial to the
original fortress-like
Atheneum structure of 1842.
Right: Architect's
rendering of the Herbert F.
Johnson Museum of Art on
the Cornell campus in
Ithaca, New York, scheduled
for completion in 1972.

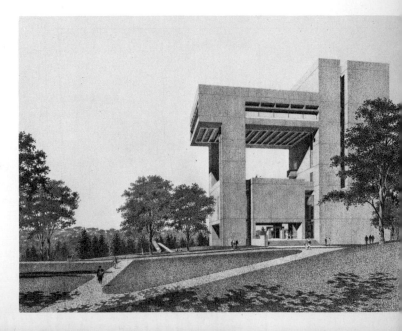

the profits from any future sales of the work at increased prices. Museum directors are often identified as principal villains in this deplorable situation. Seen as having almost dictatorial powers over the fashions of taste in art, they are accused of being insensitive parasites, living on the backs of artists, without whom there could be no museums at all. Artists themselves, it is sometimes asserted, should guide the policies and practices of museums, and museum directors should merely serve as coordinators and liaisons with money resources. The attempt to respond to these artist demands and to help resolve the related legal problems has brought many directors close to despair.

Further, the democratizing of museums has called attention to the fact that they have been oriented essentially toward white upper- and middle-class Americans. Because they have evolved largely through the efforts of the rich, museums have tended to embody the interests of the rich. If museum directors follow the policies established by their boards, as they properly should, they are often attacked as being racist and sexist. On the other hand, some boards of trustees have been oversensitive to their past sins and have instructed directors to cater to every whim of dissident groups, thus destroying the integrity and even threatening the existence of their museums. Once more the director is caught in the middle of social forces that seem to squeeze relentlessly from all sides.

Add to these pressures the necessity of pursuing at least some serious scholarly work to avoid the disdain of academic art historians, the obligations of a frantic social schedule, and the requirement of participating in endless committee meetings of various museum organizations, and you begin to have some idea of the nature of this glorious profession of directing an art museum. Faced with such an awesome array of problems, many museum directors have been driven out of the profession, if not out of their heads. Like the university president, the art-museum director sometimes seems destined for extinction, and not without cheers from several quarters.

It must be evident that I have painted the museum director as the passive target of a bewildering number of arrows from forces often in conflict among themselves. He is not really the primary target; he just happens to be in the middle of no-man's-land. Salvation for him, and perhaps for art museums, rests in his ability to resist paranoia and to realize that most of the criticisms directed at him come from extremely limited perspectives. No doubt many of the premises upon which museums were originally founded need drastic revision if museums are to maintain contact with contemporary human values. But it is also evident that museums simply cannot provide all things cultural to all people. And no museum director, no matter how astute, can possibly be in equal measure a distinguished art historian, a faultless administrator, an architectural consultant, a social lion, a friend of artists, an expert public-relations man and fund-raiser, and a practical politician.

To remain healthy a man must specialize somewhat, and his psychological set and his personal experience must guide the direction of his specialization. Similarly, the spirit and the history of an institution should guide its policy. There are signs that in some museums both the directors and the trustees are beginning to recognize that limitations are not necessarily weaknesses. Just as the country may be benefited by voluntarily foregoing world leadership in the development of the supersonic transport, so a museum may be strengthened by foregoing some of the growth and popular activities demanded by special interests. Intentional limitation and selective focusing of resources may be the key to the survival of museums as of mankind.

By this I do not mean, of course, that museums should decide merely to concentrate upon one aspect of art history, but rather that they should define limited goals with clarity and humility. One museum could be entirely dedicated to art for the people, for example, another to truly distinguished collections and scholarly exhibitions, while a third could be more oriented toward education—and there are infinite and much subtler variations possible. Ideally this definition should

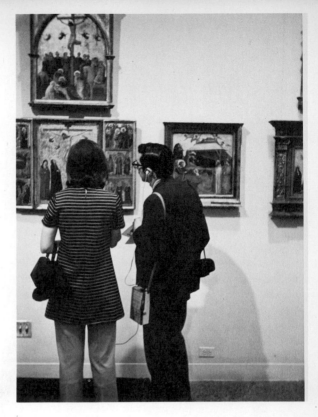

*Spectators plugged in on
the audio-guide system at the
Metropolitan Museum in New York.
Photo Nancy Foote.*

be accomplished in harmony by the trustees and the director, and if this harmony exists the goals can be agreed upon easily or even tacitly understood. With such a definition, explicit or implicit, a director can focus his efforts and develop a personal style of leadership which can make the museum a living, spiritually active place. Without some such definition, a director may be torn apart in relatively short order by demands which are often mutually exclusive. Freed from the overwhelming burden of being expected to operate in many capacities at once, a museum director can turn his creative energies to things that really matter to him and to his institution. And, seeing directors free from that burden, more and better men and women will be attracted to the profession.

Valuable as they are, the establishment of professional standards for museum workers and the enlarging of museum training programs throughout the country cannot produce superior museum directors. Standards for museum workers, like the accreditation of public school teachers, tend only to guarantee certain minimum levels of performance. No provision in them can be made, of course, for the soaring intellect, the great humanistic soul or even the lively wit one delights in finding occasionally within the directorial ranks. Though the giants of Fiske Kimball's simpler time may be gone forever, these and other valuable qualities will appear among us in greater quantity only when the profession itself attracts people who possess them. And such men and women will be attracted only when museums are no longer cultural playgrounds and human meat-grinders, when directors are able to regain a sense of direction and trustees a sense of trust.

The dilemmas of the curator EDWARD F. FRY

"With regard to the structure of society and of
social institutions, the museum curator
is very much like a secular priest or, as is
a university professor, a monk partly in
and partly out of active society . . . To the
extent that a curator deals with modern and
contemporary art, however, he is very much in the
world and bears the responsibility of knowing
not just art history, but also all the
diverse issues and disciplines of modern life."

For as long as there have been collectors and collections, curators have existed in one form or another. Before the rise of public collections and museums in the nineteenth century, the private collectors of works of art, antiquities, coins, medals, skeletons or other curiosities also served, in effect, as their own connoisseurs and curators. Only royalty, the nobility, the Church and the very wealthy maintained a "curator" for their collections; and in many cases these "curators" would spend much of their energy in the negotiation and purchase of additions to such princely collections.

When these great collections, royal, ecclesiastical or grand-bourgeois, passed into somewhat more public domain in the late eighteenth and early nineteenth centuries, they acquired in addition a new symbolic status, similar in function to that of the relics of the Christian saints and martyrs.

The objects of art—monuments, paintings, sculpture, decorative arts, armor, furniture, etc.—that had once been commissioned or taken as spoils of war were recognized as the physical embodiment of a nation's history; and in most instances these works also, through their iconography, graphically related the historical events of a nation and its people. Thus, be it the Louvre of post-Revolutionary France, the Hermitage of Soviet Russia or any other *national,* public collection, the post-aristocratic art museum functioned not only as an

Above: The Louvre, Paris. ". . . there is hardly a European collection of national cultural importance that is private, and almost every museum curator in Europe is in the employ of the state as a civil servant."

Right: The Frick Collection, New York. "That a large part of American art museums were and still remain private, not public, institutions, and that their great benefactors were rich bourgeois rather than the state, is in keeping with the symbolic function of a museum within its social context."

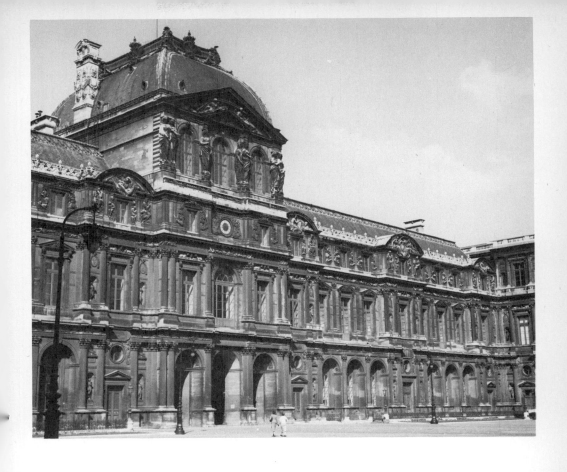

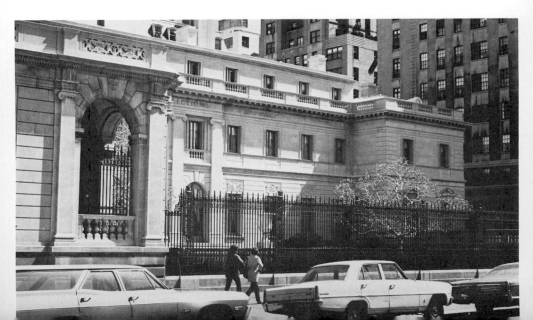

esthetic repository, but also as an educational and mythological reminder of the national heritage.

To be responsible for this physical and mythological heritage, therefore, was in itself a symbolic function, comparable in secular terms to the responsibility of a priest for the souls of his parish. Unlike the village curate, however, the museum curator (keeper in Great Britain, *conservateur* in France) was responsible not to any localized group, but to the nation as a whole. A symbolic and historical demonstration of this role is the fact that there is hardly a European collection of national cultural importance that is private, and that almost every museum curator in Europe is in the employ of the state as a civil servant. (The one seeming exception, the Vatican and the enormous artistic holdings of the Catholic church scattered throughout Europe and the world, is no exception whatsoever, because the Catholic church considers itself to be a universal state transcending secular boundaries. In this respect, it is significant that non-Catholic visitors to the Vatican or to Catholic churches and museums anywhere are expected to follow Catholic rules of comportment.)

It is this historically derived function of a museum curator that causes misunderstanding when we turn to the two situations which do not correspond to the circumstances just described. The *first* is that of the museum in a nation possessing little or nothing that it considers worth preserving as a cultural heritage. Such was the case for almost a century in the United States, and it was solved either by the purchase of European works of art or by the assembling of indigenous relics outside the fine arts, i.e., dinosaur skeletons, Indian artifacts, specimens of natural history. The purchase of an ultimately antecedent cultural heritage—European art—constitutes the history of most American museums. That a large part of American museums were and still remain private, not public, institutions, and that their great benefactors were rich bourgeois rather than the state, is in keeping with the symbolic function of a museum within its social context. For if a museum is to be both public and national, it must commemorate an indigenous cultural heritage; if, however, a museum is made up of collections transplanted by purchase from another cultural context, it remains essentially a monument to private taste and wealth.

The collecting of a cultural heritage apart from the fine arts, or sometimes in a mixed assemblage with painting and sculpture, has existed in America from a very early date. Peale's museum in Philadelphia at the beginning of the nineteenth century, combining dinosaur remains with portraits of leading American statesmen, initiated an indigenous version of the older European tradition of the "curiosity cabinet" which persisted as late as the 1950s, when the Los Angeles County Museum still housed both works of art and collections of ethnography and the natural sciences. The historical and technological collections of the Smith-

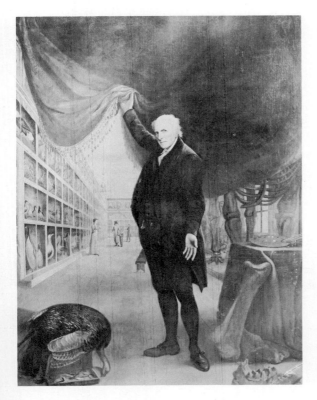

Charles Willson Peale, The Artist in His Museum *(self-portrait), oil, 1822; Pennsylvania Academy of Fine Arts, Philadelphia. "Peale's museum in Philadelphia at the beginning of the nineteenth century, combining dinosaur remains with portraits of leading American statesmen, initiated an indigenous version of the older European tradition of the 'curiosity cabinet' . . ."*

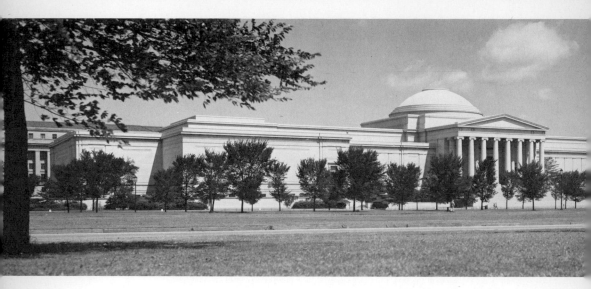

sonian Institution in Washington approach the symbolic role of a national museum preserving an indigenous heritage more closely and more revealingly than does the National Gallery of Art—which, though officially a part of the Smithsonian, has since its founding depended to an important degree on *private* munificence. (From the point of view of collecting and conserving a national heritage, Audubon was one of America's first and greatest curators, though functioning as an artist, without a museum and, ironically, with European patronage.) In an analogous fashion, the re-creation in the twentieth century of historical sites—Williamsburg, Valley Forge, Old Sturbridge—as museums and/or parks is closer in symbolic function to the role of European national museums than are many of the American museums of art filled with European purchases. This same phenomenon may be seen in a different way in Israel, where the National Museum, in a politically very young country with an able population, situated in an old and culturally rich locale, has assembled important collections of Palestinian archeology and has also actively supported contemporary art.

The *second* situation where the symbolic role of a museum and its curator differs from its original model

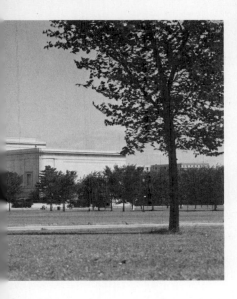

The National Gallery of Art, Washington. "The historical and technological collections of the Smithsonian Institution in Washington approach the symbolic role of a national museum preserving an indigenous heritage more closely and more revealingly than does the National Gallery of Art—which, though officially a part of the Smithsonian, has since its founding depended to an important degree on private *munificence."*

is the museum of modern and contemporary art. Here there is neither a national past to be conserved nor the mythology of cultural relics to be honored. Though at one time or another during the past one hundred years the principal center of modern art was in France, Germany, Italy, Russia or the United States, there is nevertheless a homeless and abstract character to the history of modern art that prevents it from having a stable geographical base. The locale of modern art is an immaterial state of mind which can exist anywhere. Nevertheless, museums of modern art usually establish as their symbolic basis that aspect of modern art which was most closely linked to the country in which the museum is located, i.e., Expressionism in Germany, the Paris School in France, Abstract Expressionism in America, De Stijl in Holland—and the availability of the works of course accentuates this process. A newly born national cultural heritage thus endows the museum with a symbolic social function.

Few museums of modern art totally escape this national role, so strongly rooted are the symbolic functions of museums and works of art. Those which do transcend this specific national role do so only through the substitution of a new mythological role, based on the mental constructs of modern art history. This self-referential, dialectically self-generating ideational homeland becomes the point of reference as well as the justification for the activities of modern museums and the works of art in their collections. It has only been within the last decade that this purely mythological system has begun to falter, and with it the role of modern museums. As one draws closer to the present the dilemmas of a disintegrating modern mythology undermine the cultural functions of modern museums to an increasing extent.

If we understand the diverse functions of museums, the role and the problems of the museum curator become clear. There are only three roles for a curator: (1) As the *caretaker* of the secular relics of a nation's cultural heritage, he is responsible for the preservation, documentation, promulgation and occasionally (through infrequent acquisitions) the aggrandizement of this heritage. (2) As the *assembler* of an otherwise nonexistent cultural heritage, he must acquire as many as possible of the important works representing the cultural traditions which he or his institution seeks to appropriate as a transplanted heritage. (3) As the *ideologue* operating within the history of modern art, he creates a collection demonstrating the ideational development of modernism, locates contemporary artists whose works extend and complete the mythological structure of modern art, discovers or rediscovers precedents for recent art, creates critical doctrines which legitimize new trends, and acts as a supposedly disinterested broker or catalyst between collectors, critics, publishers, dealers, architects, philanthropists and intellectuals on the one hand, and artists on the other.

All three roles of the curator—caretaker, assembler and ideologue—overlap to a certain extent, and none of the three is often found in a pure state. The caretaker is likely to be more knowledgeable about the technical aspects of conservation than the other two, but it is also probable that he has a broader sense and mastery of general history. Although the caretaker may be a connoisseur, it is less necessary a gift for him than it is to be an archivist and master of documentation. Rarely, if ever, is he called upon to exercise the skills of display and installation.

The assembler must be preeminently a connoisseur, diplomat, intelligence agent and shrewd bargainer. His abilities as art historian are less important than his connoisseurship, but he must be at least competent in problems of conservation and installation.

The ideologue must possess a mastery of art history and theory, and be unusually skilled in problems of display and installation. Since he spends as much of his time with artists as with objects, he must have tact, intuition and at least some of the gifts of a psycho-analyst. He needs the abilities of an archivist less than those of an abstract logician. Connoisseurship becomes of lessening importance as he deals with art more recent in date. The curator as ideologue must constantly update his knowledge of new art, not only within his own country but on an international basis, since the questions of chronological priority and innovation are of first importance in modern art history; and he must either justify new art ideologically or revise the mythology of modern art history in response to it.

All three roles of a curator are distinct from that of a museum director and other museum officials, although there is inevitably a certain duplication of roles. The most frequent conflicts are between curators and directors. The director, as chief executive of a museum, must formulate and carry out the policy of an institution, for which task he needs the counsel of his curators. Frequently, however, directors make decisions without curatorial consultation, as a result of which the curators find themselves charged with responsibilities alien to their own abilities and intellectual viewpoints. This practice implies a view of the curator's role as being primarily technocratic and is comparable to the unlikely situation of a university departmental chairman treating his professors as research assistants. In a small museum, however, the function of a curator and director are frequently synonymous.

It is in relation to temporary exhibitions that the museum curator is faced with his greatest problems at the present time. As opposed to the caretaking and assembling functions and their related documentary tasks, the organizing of temporary exhibitions is a frenetic and exhausting activity. When pursued over a long period, it encourages journalistic speed and superficiality, precludes the time necessary for thought and research at more fundamental levels, and so lessens the curator's intellectual and scholarly reserves.

The curator of modern and contemporary art is faced with problems encountered only rarely in other historical areas. Not the least is political and economic pressure exerted by dealers, critics, collectors and artists themselves. In an area where traditional standards of quality and historical importance cannot be easily applied the curator of modern art can resort only to the theoretical structure of modern art history, or even to sheer intuitive judgments, as means to defend his decisions. *Ad hominem* rebuttals of such judgments are always to be expected as well, for one man's theory and instinct may be considered no better than another's. Yet if a curator succeeds in establishing his point of view generally, he may eventually succumb to the glory and pride of becoming a tastemaker and in so doing render either tremendous good or harm to the continued free development of artistic culture. His only guide, therefore, in addition to art history, is his objective knowledge of his own instinctual inclinations and the corrective awareness of artistic events throughout the world rather than principally those on his own doorstep— be it New York, Paris or elsewhere. Such comparative, internationally based knowledge serves in itself as a means of gaining objectivity.

With regard to the structure of society and of social institutions, the museum curator is very much like a secular priest or, as is a university professor, a monk partly in and partly out of active society; the similarities between the curator and the professor are particularly evident in the caretaker phase of a museum's existence. To the extent that a curator deals with modern and contemporary art, however, he is very much in the world and bears the responsibility of knowing not just art history, but also all the diverse issues and disciplines of modern life. Here, however, he stands at a tremendous disadvantage in comparison with his academic counter-parts. Lacking the job security of tenure, the vacations and sabbaticals of university life, and often less well paid than his professorial equivalent, the museum curator is faced with the dilemma of overwhelming informational input with insufficient time and facilities for evaluation. The result all too often is a de facto capitulation, either to an extension of the mythologies of art history, to current art-critical doctrines, or to the related pressures of the commercial art market. In all cases, however, the curator in this dilemma is impelled toward an abdication of his own intellectual faculties in favor of a role very similar to that of a stockbroker, executing the commands and ideas of others in the manner of a technocrat. If museums are to function as one of the several objective, disinterested foci for the on-going cultural life of society, this structural dilemma must be resolved, at least to the extent of establishing parity between the museum curator and the university professor. Museums will otherwise very rapidly lose their painfully acquired effectiveness as cultural institutions in the United States and elsewhere; and, since there exist no vacuums in social structures, the cultural and economic alternatives to the museum are not attractive to contemplate.

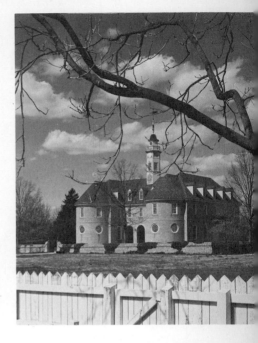

The Capitol, Colonial Williamsburg, Virginia. ". . . the re-creation in the twentieth century of historical sites—Williamsburg, Valley Forge, Old Sturbridge—as museums and/or parks is closer in symbolic function to the role of European national museums than are many of the American museums of art filled with European purchases."

No single change of present practices, however, whether it be the amelioration of professional conditions for curators or any other isolated reform, will in itself alter the unhappy situation in which museums exist today. Even a solution to the financial crises which most museums experience in the best of times would not change the fundamental problem, which is political. The immediate political difficulties facing museums under state or municipal control are self-evident, whether in Europe, Asia, South America or in the less common American examples. Visual culture easily lends itself to being used by the state as an instrument of nationalistic or ideological propaganda, whether directly through works which celebrate a nation's history or indirectly through the control of style and content in contemporary art.

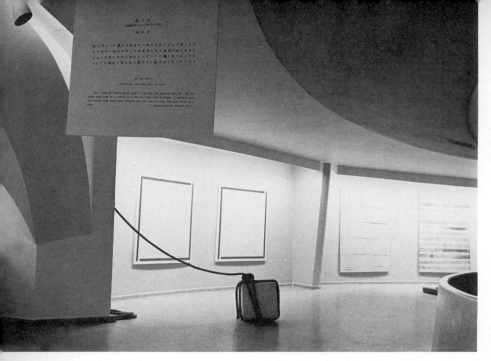

An installation view of "Contemporary Japanese Art"; Guggenheim Museum, New York, December 1970-January 1971; photo, Tatsuo Kondo. "It is in relation to temporary exhibitions that the museum curator is faced with his greatest problems at the present time. . . . the organizing of temporary exhibitions is a frenetic and exhausting activity."

The typical United States museum is privately controlled, supervised by a private board of trustees, and supported by tax-exempt endowment or gifts. Though not subject to direct state or national influence, the privately controlled American museum is as vulnerable (if not more so) to indirect political pressures as any public museum. The American tax laws, first of all, exert an indirect influence on all tax-exempt institutions by prohibiting any activity which might be construed as overtly political. This restriction is a formidable instrument of censorship in itself and encourages the retention of an outmoded mythology of estheticism and "pure" art. Recent modifications of United States laws have also threatened the tax-exempt status of foundations, a development which if pursued to its logical conclusion could eliminate the economic support they give to museums and other cultural enterprises. This possibility, in conjunction with the economic plight of museums, may cause an involuntary metamorphosis from private to public on the part of museums and other institutions, including private universities.

A far more pervasive and immediate source of political interference in private American museums is the board of trustees and the surrounding community at large. Trustees are rarely chosen unless they possess either considerable wealth or a considerable art collection (preferably both), and such individuals often find it difficult to restrain themselves from interfering with the professional operation of a museum. Under the best of circumstances, museum boards are dominated by a trustee who is the equivalent in the economic-cultural sphere of Plato's ideal philosopher-king; but the usual situation is that of wealthy yet uninformed individuals exerting control over a well-informed professional staff. The consequence in most cases is a museum which exists peacefully within its community but which does not exert a role of intellectual or cultural leadership nor of catalytic innovation.

This institutional posture of compromise and accommodation inevitably affects the professional activities of museum directors and curators as much as would an open political control on the part of the state, with the Marcusian difference that the control eventually becomes an internalized psychic mechanism rather than a set of publicly imposed restrictions. Recent challenges to the structure of authority in American private museums have yielded no viable alternatives. Artist groups, cultural radicals and militant minorities have demonstrated a greater interest in usurping a presently existing structure of economic-cultural power than in devising a more satisfactory means for museums to achieve cultural and social goals. Museums happen to be an especially conspicuous form of wealth, and the real issue in much recent conflict between museums and the public is the allocation of wealth, public or private, to acquiring art rather than to other ends. If we return, however, to the museums' various functions, we realize that in many instances the public is asking museums to do what is impossible for them. Museums in all but the largest American cities function simultaneously as repositories for local cultural relics, accumulations of works from other cultures, and as supporters of contemporary art. Collections of older art serve a symbolic and educational purpose only. It is only in the sector of contemporary art that these general museums can, like institutions devoted specifically to modern and contemporary art, function in direct relation to the ongoing life of the community.

That there is often such a divergence of function within a single institution has caused unnecessary misunderstanding; so far as contemporary art is concerned, however, museums and their curators must move simultaneously toward a greater professional autonomy and a greater involvement with the cultural and social issues of their communities. To do so will require a change in the tax laws, a generally enforced and accepted shift in the relationship between trustees and professionals, and a disbursement of public monies unaccompanied by political influence. This last requirement is not only the most difficult but also the most desirable for the forseeable future of American art museums, whether they remain private or become public institutions. It is also in keeping with the historical role of museums as they have developed in this country. For just as the separation of church and state is a fundamental tenet of the American social contract, so must there remain an equivalent separation of culture from the state. To violate this principle, as has already occurred periodically in publicly supported education, would signify an end to one of the great social experiments of modern history, and a reversion to principles and practices which have long since been discredited elsewhere.

Power
and
esthetics:
The
trustee GRACE GLUECK

"It is the board that, by setting the museum's general
policy, governs all its programs and activities.
It is the board that is responsible for
finances and the care of the museum's assets, including
its collections and physical plant. And it is
from the board—and the board alone—that the director
and his staff receive their authority to operate."

Approximately twenty thousand men and women in this country serve as trustees on the boards of more than one thousand art museums, controlling buildings and works of art worth incalculable billions. As a species, they have much in common, as revealed by a recent but unpublished cross-country sampling of 156 board members by the Twentieth Century Fund. Sixty percent were at least sixty years old and graduated from Ivy League or Little Ivy League schools; they averaged three trusteeships each in other cultural or educational institutions, and thirty-eight percent listed Episcopalian as their religion. Nearly a third were in banking and finance (with many of these holding law degrees); nearly a fifth worked in law firms, another near-fifth in the arts, architecture or the literary world, and the rest were drawn from academic fields, community organizations or business.

Though the sampling was small, it shows that trustees do have an Establishment homogeneity giving critics leverage to charge them with insensitivity to community interests. What's more, opponents aver, their undemocratic procedures in selecting fellow trustees (most museum boards are self-perpetuating) have made their museums unrepresentative of the broad constituencies they serve. Dissidents are demanding changes in the structure and outlook of museum boards. Recently in New York, for example, where trustee-baiting has become a fine art, a clutch of Metropolitan Museum board members held a dinner meeting to discuss new acquisitions in what, with curious aptness, is referred to as the Louis XVI Room. They were treated to an invasion of cockroaches, poured onto the table from a jar by members of the Art Workers Coalition. The trustees, charged the Coalitionists, were preoccupied with acquiring art rather than with communicating the spirit that produced it.

Such public recognition—however negative—is a new experience for museum boards, corporate bodies which have little tropism for the limelight. Solid citizens, pillars of the community and often prominent personalities in their own right, trustees are usually content collectively to hold the reins while their spirited horses—directors and curators—perform for the public eye.

Yet the dissidents correctly perceive the trustees' real power. It is the board that, by setting the museum's general policy, governs all its programs and activities. It is the board that is responsible for finances and the care of the museum's assets, including its collections and physical plant. And it is from the board—and the board alone—that the director and his staff receive their authority to operate.

The duties—and prerogatives—of trustees are spelled out in general terms. The constitution of the Metropolitan Museum, for example, provides that the board of trustees ". . . shall manage, preserve and protect the property of the Corporation [i.e., the museum] and shall have full and exclusive power to conduct its own affairs." The more detailed bylaws of the Museum of Fine Arts, Boston, state that the board of trustees "shall have the entire charge, control and management of the Corporation, its property and affairs and of the carrying out of all or any of its purposes and may exercise all of its powers."

Among other rights, for example, the Boston board may "appoint and, at its discretion, remove or suspend such officers, agents and employees as it from time to time thinks fit and determine their duties." It may "fix, and from time to time as it sees fit, change all salaries and other compensation." It may "appoint any officer, permanently or temporarily, to have such powers and perform such duties as it sees fit."

Under the terse legal provisions of such instruments, boards carry on a wide variety of functions. "A board's primary object is to keep the museum open and running," says Roland L. Redmond, a trustee and past president of the Metropolitan, and to that end, in the larger museums, trustee tasks are usually parceled out through a committee system. Typical committees are: (1) An Investment and/or Finance Committee, which supervises the museum's endowment holdings and plans the funding of its various expenses. The committee may also oversee the museum's business operations—its admissions and sales desk, restaurant, bookstore, auditorium, lecture series, etc. (2) A Collections and/or Acquisitions Committee, which considers the museum's acquisitions program, sometimes raising money among its own members to buy important objects (funds for the $1,400,000 Monet, *La Terrasse à Sainte-Adresse*, acquired by the Metropolitan in 1967, were reportedly rounded up by the director, Thomas Hoving, in five or six phone calls to trustees). (3) A Program Committee, which scrutinizes the museum's program, including exhibitions and educational activities. (4) Visiting committees, which keep in touch with various curatorial departments of the museum, and often act as consultants to them (some museum trustees, like the Metropolitan's Judge Irwin Untermyer, are highly knowledgeable art connoisseurs in their own right). (5) A Legal Committee, which reviews all legal questions, such as labor relations and pensions.

In carrying out its activities, a good board takes pains not to interfere with the work of the director and his professional staff. Such interference is often the precipitating cause in resignations of directors. When in 1965 the scrappy, anxious trustees of the fledgling Los Angeles County Museum of Art began to obtrude on the day-to-day operations of one of the country's outstanding museum directors, Richard F. Brown, he quit in a huff. Retaliating, they in turn charged him with administrative incompetence. From this standpoint, according to Thomas P. F. Hoving, the Metropolitan Museum "has one of the country's best boards because it allows no prima donna types to prevail. It has clearly defined its relationship with the professional staff, and it respects the chain of command."

Besides work and advice trustees may, if they choose, give art and/or money. Like most benefactors, board members tend to favor "glamor" contributions over the mundane; there is little glory in giving money to raise staff salaries or buy an air-conditioning unit. Pictures carry name tags, and building wings bear plaques. At the Museum of Modern Art, whose board includes several Rockefellers, the total trustee and nontrustee contribution toward operating expenses for 1968–69 was $340,400, with a deficit-ridden budget of $6,972,-100. Yet that same year, a five-man syndicate of trustees

*Installation view, "Four Americans in
Paris: The Collections of Gertrude Stein and
Her Family"; Museum of Modern Art, New York,
December 1970–March 1971. "At the Museum
of Modern Art . . . a five-man syndicate of
trustees and a patron . . . paid over six million
dollars for the Gertrude Stein Collection, a group
of forty-seven early works by Picasso and Gris."*

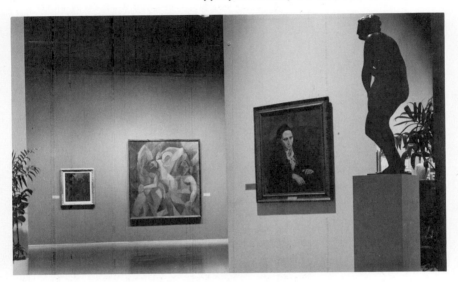

and a patron (including two Rockefeller brothers) paid
over six million dollars for the Gertrude Stein Collection,
a group of forty-seven early works by Picasso and Gris.
Five or six key pictures were pledged as gifts to the
museum; the rest are in the trustees' own collections.
Not only are the gifts tax-deductible; the holdings retained by the trustees have been enhanced in value by
a huge exhibition of the Stein Collections recently
mounted by the museum and financed not by the trustees
but by the Alcoa Foundation. (A museum spokesman
points out that four of the Stein purchasers also pledged
substantial gifts to a building-fund drive the museum
initiated that year. The pledges—only one has come
through at this writing—are redirected to endowment
funds, the museum having scrapped its building drive.)

Why are trustees chosen? For the same reason as they
were one hundred years ago, when some of this coun-

try's great museums were founded: because they are men of substance with money, business acumen and/or an interest in art, or at least a collection they can leave to the museum. Although all museums were conceived as educational in function, existing for enlightenment of the public, the "public" as such did not and still does not have much of a voice in their running. (Unless the museum is supported by public funds: The Metropolitan, for example, which gets part of its operating expenses from the city of New York, has "public" representation on its board in the form of city officials who sit ex officio; the Museum of Modern Art, entirely supported by private funds, does not.)

Today museum boards, for the most part as self-perpetuating as those of exclusive clubs, still choose their fellow members on the same basis, virtually guaranteeing that their institutions will reflect the interests of the elite. In general, trustees attend the same schools and churches, join the same clubs, marry each other, live in the same upper-crust suburbs and sit on the boards of each other's corporations. "Trustees operate in the milieu in which constant interaction with people and institutions that share their set of values reinforces a common viewpoint," notes the Twentieth Century Fund survey. "It is inevitable that they bring this viewpoint to the operation of museums."

Take, for example, the cozy board of the conservative, privately funded Cleveland Museum. Of sixteen members, no less than ten are related in some way to founders, past trustees or benefactors of the museum, to say nothing of each other. Mrs. R. Henry Norweb, the board's president, is a granddaughter of Liberty Holden, a nineteenth-century financier, collector and chairman of the museum's first building committee. Trustee James H. Dempsey, Jr., a lawyer, is married to the daughter of benefactor J. C. Bolton, and is also a partner in the law firm of Squire, Sanders and Dempsey, of which the Sanders was president of Cleveland's board in 1914–19. (The same law firm also furnished another board president, Harold T. Clark, 1950–62).

Trustee Robert I. Gale, Jr., president of the Midwest Forge Co., a prominent Cleveland industry, is married to a granddaughter of David Z. Norton, a Great Lakes shipping magnate and an early benefactor. Trustee Mrs. David S. Ingalls was May Harkness, daughter of Edward S. Harkness, a railroad magnate and museum benefactor. (The Ingallses, associated with the Taft family, have been active in Ohio Republican politics.) Trustee Paul J. Vignos, Jr., a physician, is married to Mrs. Ingalls' daughter.

Trustee James D. Ireland is a nephew of William G. Mather, nineteenth-century Cleveland industrialist, collector and former board president. Trustee Severance A. Millikin is a nephew of John L. Severance, a Cleveland industrialist (Standard Oil), collector and former board president. Trustee A. Dean Perry, a stockbroker and collector of Chinese paintings, is married to Helen Wade Greene, a granddaughter of Jephtha Wade, donor of the land on which the museum is built. Trustee James N. Sherwin is the husband of Kathleen Burke, daughter of Edmund S. Burke, a museum benefactor. Trustee Lewis C. Williams is the son of Lewis B. Williams, a collector, donor and former trustee.

Of the remaining six, three are connected in some way with business firms whose founding families were museum benefactors. Ralph S. Schmitt is ex-president of the Cleveland Twist Drill Co., John S. Wilbur is executive vice-president of the Cleveland Cliffs Iron Co., and Mrs. Alfred M. Rankin is married to a director of the Oglebay Norton Co., the lake shipping firm founded by David Z. Norton.

And of the board's three "outsiders," none lacks Establishment credentials: George P. Bickford, a lawyer and prominent Republican; Willis B. Boyer, president of the Republic Steel Corp.; and Rabbi Daniel J. Silver, son of the well-known Cleveland rabbi, Abba Hillel Silver, and the board's only minority-group member.

Cleveland, of course, is an extreme example of the interlocking structure of museum boards; but even the members of other, less exclusive boards have what might be called a solid community of interests. The board of the Museum of Fine Arts in Boston (on ,which city representatives sit) is studded with Old Boston names like Cabot, Coolidge, Gardner and Lowell; of its twenty-

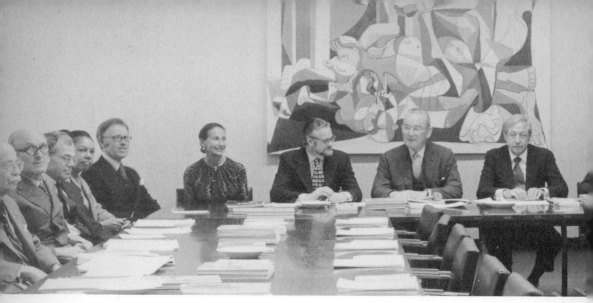

*A recent meeting of the
board of trustees at the
Museum of Modern Art, with
seventeen of the current
forty members. Left to
right: Ranald H. Macdonald,
Philip Johnson, Robert R.
Barker, Dr. Mamie Phipps
Clark, Gifford Phillips,
Mrs. Armand P. Bartos,
Richard H. Koch (staff
officer), John Hay Whitney,
William S. Paley, John
B. Hightower, John
de Menil, Mrs. Frank Y.
Larkin, J. Frederic
Byers III, Mrs. Walter
Hochschild, Mrs. John D.
Rockefeller III, Mrs.
Donald B. Straus, Dr.
Clifton R. Wharton, Jr.,
Mrs. Alfred R. Stern.*

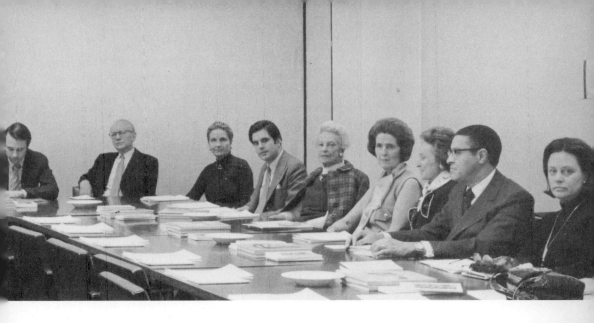

To be a trustee, you must have wealth, wisdom or works of art.
   Anonymous.

A trustee is a sacred cow that has to be milked on occasion.
   Francis Henry Taylor, director, Metropolitan Museum of Art, 1940–54.

My idea of a great trustee is Tom Hoving.
   Thomas P. F. Hoving, director, Metropolitan
   Museum of Art, who as Parks Commissioner
   served ex officio on a number of boards.

My ideal trustee is Thomas Jefferson—intellectual, wealthy, polite, humanitarian.
   John Hightower, director, Museum of Modern Art.

A trustee should put up and shut up.
   Director of a small museum.

seven active trustees, more than half attended (or are married to those who attended) Harvard. Two trustees, George Peabody Gardner and John L. Gardner, are father and son; another, Walter Muir Whitehill, is married to the sister of trustee John Coolidge. The fathers of trustees Nelson W. Aldrich and George P. Gardner sat on the board before them, as did the brother of William A. Coolidge before *him*.

The twenty-six-man board of the Art Institute of Chicago has two McCormicks (Brooks McCormick, president of the International Harvester Co., and Bowen Blair, son of William McCormick Blair, the museum's president), plus such other scions of famous benefactors as Potter Palmer and Marshall Field. The Museum of Modern Art has three Rockefellers on its board (or almost, since John D. III is represented by his wife, Blanchette). Another family team also serves here: board president William S. Paley, chairman of the board of CBS, and his son-in-law, J. Frederic Byers III.

Not only are museum trustees connected on their individual boards; they sometimes serve on the boards of other museums or are related by family or business connections to trustees of other museums. At the Museum of Modern Art, for example, trustee Mrs. C. Douglas Dillon is the wife of the president of the Metropolitan Museum; trustee Mary Lasker is the stepmother of Mrs. Leigh B. Block, a trustee of the Chicago Art Institute, and of Mrs. Sidney Brody, wife of the president of the board of the Los Angeles County Museum. Trustee John Hay Whitney also serves as vice-president of Washington's National Gallery of Art; trustee John de Menil is a trustee of the Museum of Fine Arts in Houston, the Amon Carter Museum in Fort Worth and the Museum of Primitive Art in New York City.

At the Metropolitan, trustee John R. H. Blum is also a trustee of the Brooklyn Museum and president of the Brooklyn Institute of Arts and Sciences, its parent body. Trustee André Meyer, a patron of the Museum of Modern Art Collections, was instrumental in the Stein Collection purchase there.

This is not, of course, to say that boards, as they are

presently constituted, are unsuited to run the institutions they govern, as *they* are presently constituted. As long as museums are not government-supported (only a handful are) they need financiers and fund-raisers on their boards. As long as they are in the collecting business, they need wealthy and expert acquisitors—although, in the case of less-established museums, this can be a two-edged sword. The acquisitions of Norton Simon, tycoon trustee of the L.A. County Museum of Art, have given him a considerable hold on the young museum, which can scarcely afford to enter the prohibitively priced field of Renaissance and Impressionist art and relies greatly on his loans to fill its galleries.

The trouble is that most such trustees tend to be far less interested in the educational and "community" side of their museums than in their collecting and curatorial aspects. Oriented as they are to think of their museums as encyclopediae of great objects, storehouses for art of the past, they are notoriously slow to recognize what may be more pressing public interests. This is aptly illustrated by the case of the Lehman Collection, a magnificent private holding of more than three thousand objects of Western European Art, left to the Metropolitan by its late board chairman, Robert Lehman, and posthumously accepted with great fanfare by his fellow trustees.

This irresistible collection, which for many cities would comprise a well-stocked museum in itself, has strings attached; it must be preserved forever as an entity —which has necessitated the planning of a special wing. Designed as part of the Met's new Master Plan, the Lehman Pavilion has sparked a public furor, with opponents contending that it encroaches on Central Park and that the Met, already in danger of becoming an "art palace" like the Louvre, should place the collection in some other area where art facilities are scarce.

The Met has no intention of complying. According to one Old Guard trustee, "Our real mistake is that we didn't accept the collection quietly." Nevertheless, the public outcry over this, and other Met projects, has given the board pause. Recently, "radically reinterpreting its role in serving the broader community," the

Met has instituted a series of local programs, sending exhibition materials to branch libraries and other facilities in the boroughs, holding a series of "borough" open houses at the museum, and developing an Advisory Board of "representatives of all elements of the New York City community to aid the Museum in finding ways to serve the community."

The Met is not alone in responding to public pressure; a drive toward broader board representation is evident throughout the country. The Museum of Modern Art, for example, a WASP-oriented establishment for many years, has slowly been diversifying its representation. This past year, to "broaden the range of interests and special talents represented," the board increased its size by one-third (to forty), electing more educators, more women, more businessmen, more representatives of ethnic groups and, for the first time, blacks: Dr. Mamie Clark, a psychologist and wife of the social psychologist Dr. Kenneth Clark; and Clifton R. Wharton, Jr., the brilliant president of Michigan State University.

Not only that; brooding about the future, the board established two unprecedented committees: an "Ad Hoc Committee on the Contemporary Meaning of Art and the Role of the Museum of Modern Art," and a "Committee for the Study of Afro-American, Hispanic and other Ethnic Art."

To the surprise of many Coast-watchers, the Los Angeles County Museum of Art, loaded with powerful industrialists, has just elected its first black trustee, Charles Z. Wilson, Jr., vice-chancellor of academic programs and professor of education at UCLA, and taken the daring step of adding an artist, William Brice, a professor in the UCLA art department.

And although Thomas Hoving noted publicly at a City Council hearing some months ago that his efforts to get the Metropolitan's board to elect more ethnic representatives had been fruitless, at this writing the board has made a resolution—admittedly not earth-shaking—to broaden its representation by allocating five seats at its thirty-five-man table to "persons from the four boroughs outside of Manhattan."

But there is pressure for more radical change, and not only from young dissidents. In a recent *Art News* issue devoted to the Metropolitan Museum, the art historian Meyer Schapiro urged a change in the composition of the Met's board to include representatives of the museum's membership. Pointing out that the twenty-five thousand members contribute annually about $450,000—more than the trustees—he notes that they include "artists, teachers, scholars and collectors, as well as amateurs in the old sense; their judgment in matters of art, their awareness of public needs, is probably as informed and serious as the trustees."

He also urges a voice on the board for the community, since it contributes each year, through the city's budget, a substantial portion of the Met's total operating income. As precedent, he cites the fact that other institutions, such as private universities, have increasingly opened their governing boards to alumni representatives, and have consulted faculty and students in the nomination of trustees.

With 90 percent of museums in this country unable to meet their operating costs, funding will have to come more and more from public and corporate sources—and proposals such as these may not be far from implementation. Even Old Guard trustees can see the handwriting on the wall—that the cozy, clubby era of museums as private fiefs is over. Trustees in the future will have to earn their places on the boards by more than money and the magic of family name.

The university museum: Accidental past, purposeful future?

JOHN R. SPENCER

"College and university art museums have
arrived at their present position
through a series of accidents,
but accidents need not control their
future existence. The peculiarly
American concept of the art museum as
a means of education brought them into
being and determined the direction
of their growth. Their desire to emulate
the large city museums has raised
a few to enviable heights
but will lead only to frustration for
the greater majority." . . . But
they have a more important role
to play than they have yet recognized.

University and college art museums are such ill-used, undernourished and overlooked entities that one is tempted to consider them a product of chance. Their very existence is characterized by contradiction. They are often considered a showplace or the symbol of culture on campus, and yet a recent report has encouraged university administrators to balance their budgets by making the first cuts in "cultural activities"—presumably the visual as well as the performing arts. New campus art museums are coming into existence at an alarming rate at just the moment when works of art and funds to buy them are becoming increasingly hard to find. Chance may have midwifed these museums and chance may have determined their number, but chance will not extricate them from the problems they now face.

There are so many of them. In 1966 HEW counted 130 campus museums devoted solely to art and an additional thirty-six devoted to art and something else. Although these outdated figures are not staggering, they emphasize the scope of the problem. Not only do these museums comprise one-third of all the art museums in the United States, but they also make up approximately one-half of all college and university museums of all types. Because they are so difficult to categorize, the Belmont report touched only briefly on college and university art museums. Annual budget does not apply as it does to "standard" art museums, for their budget is confused and complex. Moreover, the richest collection may be found in the university museum with the smallest acquisition budget. These museums range, in their holdings, all the way from a large number of quality works of art down to a handful of donations and works by local artists or no collection at all. The standard criterion of attendance fails to apply as well, for the number of potential visitors to a campus museum is already restricted.

Although college and university museums are so diverse that they are difficult to categorize, they share certain problems and differ from other art museums in specific ways. Whether the university museum is a part of the "crisis on campus" or is in a crisis all its own is not clear. The directors of these museums, however, have been questioning and attempting to identify those elements that have created the situation in which they now find themselves. Some of the problems have been created by the history of the college and university museum, some by its environment and some by the university museum's definition of itself and its role.

The origins of the college and university art museum are different from those of all other museums. Unlike scientific and historical museums and unlike national or civic art museums, they have no real European model. They were founded not as an aid to research, not for the glory of the nation or of a city, but to educate the young. Nor were they, like the Metropolitan Museum, founded to provide "innocent and refined enjoyment," but to encourage hard intellectual effort. The few European university art collections were founded mainly by chance and not with the avowed purpose of making art a part of undergraduate life. The concept of art as a humanistic educative tool probably goes all the way back to Leon Battista Alberti, but the role of art in education as it exists today is in great part due to Rousseau and Ruskin. When Colonel Trumbull gave his collection to Yale in 1832, he was certainly thinking first of an annuity for Colonel Trumbull, but Silliman and others were clearly aware of the educational possibilities of the historical paintings. Yale acquired the Jarves collection for its educational value after it had been refused by the Boston and Metropolitan museums. Until recent years most college and university art museums have consciously or unconsciously followed the Yale pattern in a desire to expand education into all areas subject to the availability of an inexpensive collection. As a result many museums at some point in their history have resembled the Yale museum of about 1870, with a strong desire to teach and precious little to teach with. Italian "primitives" and American historical paintings are hardly an adequate introduction to the history of art. Hence the scramble to fill gaps and to make do with plaster casts or prints until "real" works of art could be acquired. Education, however, has remained dominant, overriding the acquisitive drives of the museum staff, and finding eternal expression at the entrance of the campus museum in lapidary phrases.

The environment of the university museum has rendered it schizoid. It does not know whether it is an art museum among art museums or an educational institution. All university museums desire to emulate the large civic museums to some degree. They set the same professional standards for their staffs and for their collections that they have observed in the large museums. They know they are poor cousins who cannot compete in acquisition, so they buy equivalents or attempt to anticipate trends in taste by buying against the market. They cannot mount major exhibitions, so they rent package shows. They are always flattered to lend to a large museum, though it means temporarily depriving themselves of one of their greatest attractions and even though there is small chance that the favor of a loan will be returned. Privately they congratulate themselves that they are not required to maintain such a large educational staff as the major museums, but in every other way they attempt to catch some of the reflected glory of being like these major museums. Unfortunately, the closer the university museum approaches this model, the farther it is removed from its home university.

The university environment works a subtle change on the campus museum unknown in municipal or private institutions. The staff of the museum is difficult to classify in the university table of organization. It is not clear whether they are to be ranked with librarians, technical assistants or teaching faculty. So far as rank and salary are concerned they are generally less well-off than their colleagues in the nonuniversity museums, and they generally rank well below teaching faculty with comparable training and experience. The university itself is in large part responsible for the attitude that casts the museum staff in a second-class role. Traditionally, the graduate schools have considered museum work inferior to teaching and regard the Ph.D. as overtraining for a museum career. Fortunately, this attitude is changing. The universities have also tended to think of the art museum or gallery as a peripheral operation that consumes funds but does not

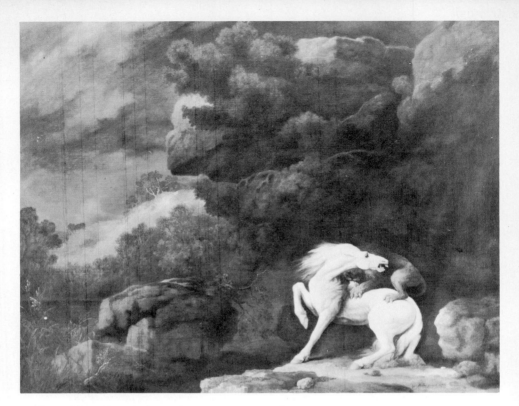

produce. There is no circulation count as in a library and no body count as in a department to indicate success. Funds available for staff, exhibitions or acquisitions therefore receive low priority in the university budget.

In the same way donors are generally restricted to alumni and university trustees (also alumni) whose collections are often characterized by their modesty and timidity. There are obvious exceptions, but major donations to college or university museums in the last ten years can be counted on the fingers of one hand. However, the university does provide the museum with an audience that no other museum enjoys. This audience has already been conditioned to a high degree of tolerance and curiosity. They will neither giggle nor blush at pornography; they will not threaten to cancel donations, or write irate letters to the editor. On a proportional basis a university museum can count on a larger attendance at an exhibition of Netherlandish Mannerist goldsmith designs than can a large city

George Stubbs, Lion Attacking a Horse, *oil, 1770; Yale University Art Gallery, New Haven, Connecticut. Gift of Yale University Art Gallery Associates, 1955.*

museum. The receptivity of this audience is due solely to the existence of the museum on a campus, to the educational environment provided by the university.

The university environment works other changes upon its art museum, because of a compartmentalization of teaching if not of knowledge. Every one of these museums or galleries is, or at some point in its history was, attached to an art department. The museum then becomes an extension of or an ancillary function for the art department. All other faculties of the university are rigorously excluded except as passive observers. A museum exhibition with sociological implications, for example, or one designed to demonstrate the art in science, except on a superficial level, is rare. The museum tends either to be subservient to the art department or to rival it. Rarely do the two achieve a level of equality and mutual cooperation. Where the art-history department dominates, the collection tends to become full-scale, full-color illustrations of the historical periods taught. Art-historically oriented curators bring previously acquired knowledge to bear upon an object rather than becoming so curious about an object that they desire to acquire knowledge about it. Where the studio department dominates, the museum serves to exhibit the work of the teaching faculty and selected students or, if it has an acquisition budget, to reflect the tastes of the department in contemporary art. Where the museum attempts to rival or surpass the department and the university, it fails in the educative role for which it was founded.

However, despite its many problems on a campus, the university art museum enjoys a certain sheltered status that few museums have attempted to exploit. The campus art museum is not only an acceptable place to abandon a prospective faculty member or prospective student for an hour, but it is an important symbol for the university. It represents in highly visible form the university's respect for cultural traditions. It is a symbol of continuity and of man's least-understood activity. Only on a college or university campus are those things that are not understood, are dimly understood or are totally misunderstood respected, questioned, tolerated or ignored but never feared. Such an atmosphere provides the campus art museum with opportunities unknown to other art museums.

If the college or university art museum is a product of its own history and its own peculiar environment, its present status and the kind of thinking emanating from it are due in large part to its involuntary self-description. Since no college or university museum, to my knowledge, has attempted a clear definition of itself and since the group is so disparate, it is perhaps unfair and unwise to attempt a definition. Some sort of a tentative definition of the group can be made by noting the behavior patterns of the group.

It would appear that a college or university art museum is a large museum in miniature. It has the same desire to expand the collection, "to fill gaps," to increase staff, to attract donors and to preserve and protect the works of art entrusted to it. The college or university museum is overtly dedicated to teaching, unlike the large art museum where education is a subsidiary or at best a corollary function. From this it derives that the campus museum should collect the finest examples available, it should exhibit what is taught and it should emphasize the didactic, even at the expense of the visual. It must serve the university that gives it being. It should be devoted to the on-campus group, the U-people of the community and sometimes to the alumni. It should be something like the campus library, only noncirculating and with a slower retrieval rate of stored information. With certain additions and deletions this definition would encompass all but a few college art museums.

Such a narrow concept of self has been highly restrictive in the development of these museums. It has, by implication, created hierarchies and artificial criteria for assigning each museum its appropriate place on the scale. Naturally, each museum struggles or yearns for a higher position in the order. This narrow view has also created a series of automatic responses to often repeated stimuli. An increase in attendance will solve one problem, a special exhibition will solve another, a specific kind of acquisition yet a third, and so on.

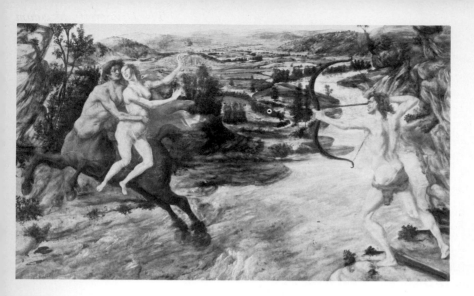

Antonio Pollaiuolo, Hercules and Deianira, *egg tempera and oil, c. 1475; Yale University Art Gallery, New Haven, Connecticut. Purchased from James Jackson Jarves in 1871.*

Unfortunately the narrow view sometimes seems to perpetuate the traditional response even when the stimuli have changed. The narrow definiton of the college and university art museum is no longer adequate to the situation. On a number of campuses a few isolated responses to the peculiar problems of the university art museum today have begun to emerge. They are not universally applicable, but they begin to point the way.

First of all, the definition of a college or university art museum must be expanded. Each museum should exist on its own unique terms. One Harvard, one Yale, one Berkeley, one Bob Jones is quite enough. There is no need for a series of pale replications of what are already prime objects. If the university art museum is truly devoted to teaching and does not already have a large collection, then there is a clear need for a coherent and balanced collection limited to one or two areas. Where the university museum can best serve as an exhibition and teaching gallery using faculty and student work, more can be achieved by a stimulating installation than by a permanent collection. In some cases a university museum might well serve as a collecting and disbursing agency for *expendable* works of art. The university can move into certain high-risk areas with greater impunity than can the university art museum; yet it is just possible that loans from the museum, or even a subsidiary collection to these areas, can make the greatest impact. Other periods have consumed the art of their time through an excess of affection. Our own time need not be different. Art museums have tended to think in very narrow terms in defining themselves and their function. This should not be. Each museum should consider carefully its place in the university, the community and the region and then set its goals for its own unique situation. A greater diversity is needed in university art museums rather than homogeneity.

Colleges and universities would also do well to ask themselves just what is meant by a "teaching museum." On campus it may be defined as a museum where one teaches, but off campus or in the dealer's gallery the term becomes a pejorative used to describe any inferior collection of inferior objects. Neither definition seems wholly accurate. The term cannot mean that one teaches solely from originals, since this is patently impossible. Frequently it means that one teaches with equivalents— Cross stands for Seurat, Giampetrino for Leonardo, a Rembrandt etching for a Rembrandt painting. There is some serious question that these equivalents really work outside the mind of the instructor or of the curator who defines them. It might be pedagogically more sound to dust off and repair the old plaster casts in the basement. Assuming that the art museum does have some sort of a collection, the next question is how does one teach? The founders of university art museums failed to write the answer into the articles of foundation, and no one seems yet to have discovered the answer. Colonel Trumbull implied that the teaching would be done by osmosis, but it is hard to believe that the Yalies of 1832 were any more patriotic, historical-minded or art-conscious than their equivalents at Harvard. Some teaching is undoubtedly achieved by immersing the student in works of art, but the degree and the rate of absorption are exceedingly difficult to measure. Traditionally, collections have been arranged in chronological sequence in order to teach by implication. The arrangement is tedious but not wholly without merit. An antidote to chronology has been clever juxtapositions of dissimilar works of art that have only been understood by those students who have completed Art A1A. Explanatory labels are blatantly pedagogical and visually distracting. Each of the traditional methods of teaching or of self-education before the work of art has some inherent flaw, but there is no simple answer. Each museum has only its own collection and a few loans to work with. How it arranges that collection—to teach by word, image or juxtaposition—depends on whether it wishes to establish the history of art, to raise esthetic or formal questions or to emphasize differences and similarities of techniques. Finally, each museum must define for itself the limits of its audience. In some cases the museum will necessarily restrict itself to the on-campus audience. In others it will feel compelled to reach out to the whole or a segment of the community or the region.

In attempting to expand the potential audience of the university museums, some directors have noted that involvement with the community often leads to community involvement with the museum, often with disastrous results. The stakes may be worth the risk, especially if ways can be found to hedge the bet. Schoolchildren of all ages form one area of expansion. Hordes of little children troop through college and university museums every year, but there is rarely an exhibition or a group of works of art arranged specifically for them. They are treated often as small adults with a lower threshold of boredom who need to hear stories. Actually they comprehend color and form much more readily than adults and need examples that will heighten and broaden that innate sensitivity. Some exhibitions should be designed to go to the schools, either to hang in rooms and corridors or to be passed from hand to hand until they are totally consumed. People of all ages love to touch. Perhaps certain works of art should be designated as "feelies" for the sighted, much as certain works have been reserved for the blind at Raleigh and Toledo. Audiences seem to want a more personal rapport with the museum. Exhibitions designed for certain groups and a change in the atmosphere of the museum will help. Most of our college museums have about as much charm as a bank vault and certainly less character. Often a visitor does not feel comfortable in an art museum, as hushed tones and the best behavior indicate. Our college and university museums do not need to take on the atmosphere of a coffeehouse or of a discotheque in order to survive, but a less forbidding and cold interior in very many instances would help to attract and to hold these new audiences.

There has been growing cooperation between museums in the last few years. The University of New Mexico and other Southwestern museums have formed a consortium to schedule traveling exhibitions. Block booking permits the exhibition to travel relatively short distances between these university museums instead of moving back and forth across the United States between each booking. The advantages to the museums and to the works of art in the exhibition are obvious. Some university museums are already arranging indefinite loans to each other. The criterion here should be utility rather than value or number. Ten Rembrandt prints for one nineteenth-century American landscape could be a fair exchange depending on the needs and collections of the museums involved. In the same way it may be possible, if the rules

Jean Auguste Dominique Ingres, Odalisque with a Slave, oil on panel, 1837; Fogg Art Museum, Harvard University, Cambridge, Massachusetts. Bequest of Grenville L. Winthrop, 1943.

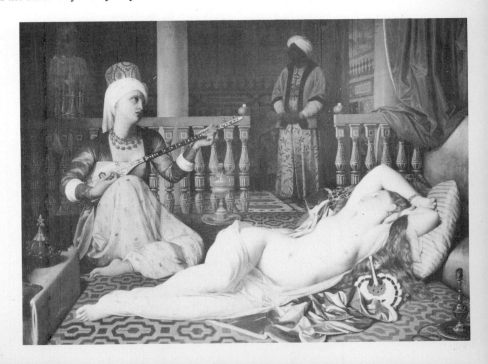

governing state institutions can be warped a little, for university museums to cooperate in the acquisitions and sharing of a major work of art. New consortia for the conservation of works of art are already in the planning stage. It has been said that most college and university museum curators are only presiding over the gradual disintegration of their collections. Clearly very few university museums can afford a full-time conservator, his laboratory and assistants, but the model of the Inter-museum Conservation Association has demonstrated that cooperation between university, city and private museums does work. Rising prices for works of art, budgets for staff and maintenance will require more rather than less cooperation among university art museums if they are to survive at all.

Many college and university art museums have been hampered by the lack of breadth in their staff and in the art department to which they are allied. Although it is severely limiting, they quite rightly buy only what they teach, for they lack the expertise to consider other areas. Unfortunately the best buys for a small museum lie in precisely those areas that are least taught in the university. Pre-Columbian art, the art of the Pacific islands, small bronzes of all periods, prints, drawings and photographs are frequently ignored for lack of knowledge. Vassar, among others, has established a kind of visiting committee made up of experts outside the college through which the museum has been able to acquire at small cost works of art that might not otherwise have been considered. Here again the university art museum must reach outside itself if it is to function adequately.

College and university art museums have arrived at their present position through a series of accidents, but accident need not control their future existence. The peculiarly American concept of the art museum as a means of education brought them into being and determined the direction of their growth. Their desire to emulate the large city museums has raised a few to enviable heights, but will lead only to frustration for the greater majority. The overwhelming desire to build a collection at any cost makes the campus art museum a convenient dumping ground for unscrupulous collectors and overly ambitious college administrators. In this case a bad collection is worse than no collection, for to educate the young badly is worse than to educate them not at all. College and university museums have a captive audience not enjoyed by any other art museum. They have a certain reputation and sometimes authority on campus. Few have attempted to exploit the strength of their position. Few have recognized the resources available to them. They have a much larger audience than they imagine and a more important role to play in the region than they have yet recognized. By breaking out of the stereotype of the campus museum, by finding what they can do best in their region, they can create a future directed by reason rather than chance.

The contemporary museum: Under the corporate wing

MAX KOZLOFF

"Regardless of whether there are any
or enough artists worth being
shown, regardless of a community's
consciousness of or interest in
art, regardless of a people's social
priorities, museum buildings sprout
up to adorn the pride of the
colorless ruling classes. In that sense,
they are no different from the moon
shots, although requiring far less
national expenditure."

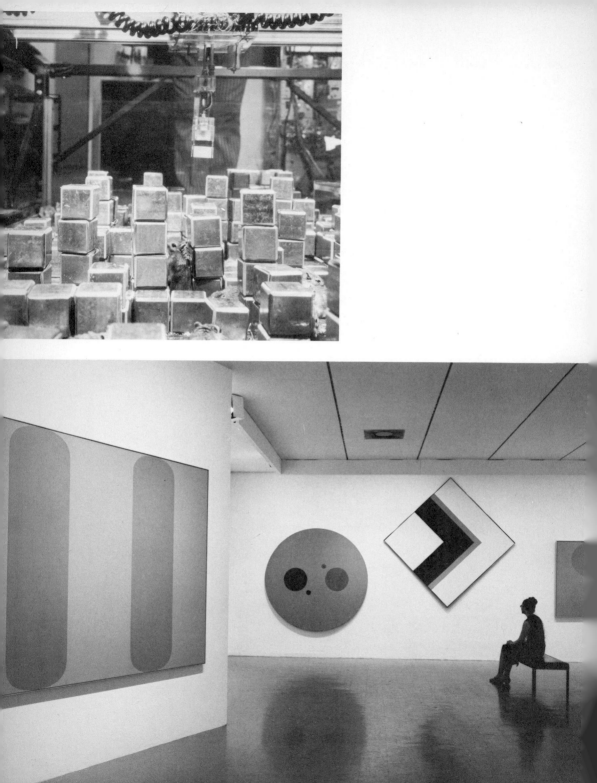

Museums of modern art have had a remarkable career. They have their predicaments now; their futures are uncertain. But it rarely occurs to us to think of them as places that have been with us only a very short time. Especially brief has been their tenure as arbiters in the reception of serious contemporary art. The great collections, the amassed treasures, yes, these are the images conjured by thoughts of the museums. But how long has anyone been accustomed to accept them as big news-breakers on the "scene"? Best to make the answer less than ten years.

In the early sixties (if one excludes the New Talent shows at the Museum of Modern Art and the Annuals at the Whitney), the American art museum came to vie with every other medium as a perpetrator of the avant-garde. It actually dared to *introduce* a sensibility still wet behind the ears. With its prestige as a cultural fixture, its resources and its huge audiences, the museum emerged as a most formidable instrument for rehearsing the myth of perpetual renewal in visual art.

To obtain some idea of the ascendance of the museum in this role, think of the comparable institution in music, the symphony orchestra. The destiny of modern music in our concerts has not been the same as that of recent art in the museums. That the symphony has become a warehouse of past musical monuments, that there is no serious recent music the concert patrons will tolerate, justly or not, is almost the reverse of what happened in art. Difficult modern music has had to retreat to the university; difficult modern art enjoyed great publicity and a bull market. The museums had a share in this.

Above: Installation view, "Seek," Nicholas Negroponte and the Architecture Machine Group, M.I.T.; Jewish Museum, New York, September–November 1970. Forty furry gerbils disarrange 2,000 plastic cubes while a mechanical grappler rearranges the cubes to hem in the animals. Museums have seized upon "practitioners of exotic media . . . .or the yeomen of technologically oriented art projects who have been corralled to illustrate various arbitrary themes." Below: Installation view, "The Responsive Eye"; Museum of Modern Art, New York, February–April 1965. This exhibition "became notorious for having inadvertently . . . given birth to far more art than it had earlier noticed or intended to foster."

Even the critics and artists earlier in the "know" than the curators eventually came to rely on the museum show as a shaper of art history. They adopted a reactive attitude to a phenomenon for which they were largely responsible in the first place. Moreover, as it took longer to organize these surveys of current "movements," realignments of artistic styles would precede the openings awaited with such expectation. "The Responsive Eye" exhibition at the Museum of Modern Art became notorious for having inadvertently, by the fact of its very announcement, given birth to far more art than it had earlier noticed or intended to foster.

Expectation lends great spirit to any artistic moment. But it was poorly understood at these gala openings how much they inaugurated a curious pile-up of energies. The production, the momentum, the turnover which they stimulated in the art world began to outpace the capacities of the museums to keep tabs on their new-found domain of art in process. Particularly as staffs and expenses grew in order to honor projections based on earlier commitments, the result was not greater versatility and flexibility in the mounting of shows, but exactly the opposite. Catalogues came out dismally late, and the time lapse between underground and "official" reputations began to lengthen again. It was a period when even short intervals were freighted with importance, and yet seemed to speed by. (Interestingly, some journalists in the press complained that Jasper Johns, at thirty-four, was much too young to have his retrospective at the Jewish Museum.)

Additionally, the various institutions, at least in New York, began to compete fiercely with each other for whatever was cresting at the moment. Little did they realize that they were also conspiring mightily to dissolve that moment. Too much, literally, was chasing too little. The artistic pickings were growing thinner. It was a hectic, halcyon decade. And it proved that nothing fails like success.

These observations on the past have already been made by a number of writers. It remains to examine the altered circumstances in which we find ourselves *now*.

The one that stands out immediately, and with which we can begin, is the *decreased* status of a museum showing for an artist.

With the exception of those geographic surveys whose spread may have extended beyond the purlieus of the New York establishment, the meaning of being in one of those shows was that one had more or less "arrived," in the vulgar sense. The endorsement provided the artist by the museum's exhibiting or buying his art added the finishing touch to earlier advances or encouragements, of which it was the orthodox climax. The commercial prospects of those so anointed might still be unsettled or reversible, but at least it could be said that a graduation had taken place, and that a group of aspirants had passed through the ranks of obscurity. Whether he was approved or not by a majority of the concerned, the artist enjoying his first participation in a museum show was a tolerably well-known figure to initiates. To some extent he had already been processed by rumor and reviews. His name had been on the lips of scouts. The system was functioning.

Nowadays, however, there are people to be seen in shows of contemporary art who have not been previously certified by anyone, who come from nowhere or anywhere, and who have had no or little previous contact with the art reward system. No bibliography exists on their work; few galleries display it. Moreover, these absolute or comparative unknowns are not presented to us as potential heroes of innovation. They are not singled out as the forerunners or even prominent figures of a movement. Rather, they are practitioners of exotic media, specialists in logic, or the yeomen of technologically oriented art projects who have been corralled to illustrate various arbitrary themes. If an exhibition of plastics is to be ballyhooed, a search is extended to discover the likeliest exponents of the latest plastic materials. The theme casually determines the variations. And the aim of such currently bandied terms as software and information art is partially to introduce a variety of strains and breeds in a field, rather than to highlight what might be the salient esthetic intentions that distinguish it—or its drift away from the esthetic. There has been a deflation of the claims advanced for any new show, accompanied by a correspondingly atomized and de-individuated roster of exhibitors. And the volume of this new kind of business, appropriately enough, symptomizes the esthetics of diffusion and the leveling of ideas to which overproduction has inevitably led. For, as in the supermarket, the multiplication of brand names does not, past a certain point, indicate a differentiation of products: in fact, it tends to demonstrate the contrary.

Once again, such phenomena are familiar enough. But in coping or not coping with them, the art-world apparatus is seriously modifying itself. For example, the critic-dealer arrangement, which has lasted about a hundred years, is giving every indication of exhaustion. Whatever its merits in the past, it is proving uneconomical and ineffective from the point of view of the thousands of careers that can no longer be channeled or treated by it. Critics and dealers acted as blackballers of, and bonding agents for, the artist. At all times they comprised a quota-conscious, self-absorbed, endlessly subjective and erratically personalized coterie of men and women. It is quite true that their often genuine enthusiasm for modern art instilled confidence and even went far to build a mainstay collector class. But present conditions make these inner circles look like congestion centers rather than catalysts.

The profession of artist today no longer manages itself very well by unofficial consensus and outdated standards of "quality." We see, rather, a breaking-down of the elite structure which had oriented its goals. In their place issues a chaotic momentum whose political animus is outgrowing its esthetic allegiances. As each day passes, it is harder to think of current art as an enclave of privately supported yet disinterested creators who are granted various degrees of lofty status by cliques of trendy intellectuals. (All that still goes on, of course, but with considerably diminished élan.) On the contrary, art now may have to survive either by becoming a publicly subsidized and manipulated cultural function (an offshoot of corporate charity) or—by turning itself into a quasi-mystical, down-and-out life style pursued by droves of young who reject the establishment and serious ambition in about equal measure.

Several rebuttals may be raised at this point. Can we not say, for instance, that artistic accomplishment triumphs over, or often has little to do with, grubby forms of patronage? It certainly does. And is it not true that many artists are forming cooperatives, setting up their own warehouse galleries, and reconnecting with their communities—in short, finding economic alternatives to the system while at the same time continuing to perform as professionals? Indeed, to their credit, they frequently do. And finally, are not universities and art schools nourishing new generations of artists with the humanist discipline that has hitherto sustained the modern tradition?

That is surely going too far. It is precisely in the schools that the political dilemma of art is made vivid. On the one hand, the teaching staff (aside from that portion of it for whom doing art is secondary to instruction) has a problematic relationship with a restricted market. The demand for what the artist in academe creates runs far short of his capacity to produce it, so that while he is given a comfortable academic salary, he is alienated from information, sanction, outlet and patronage—in short, the normally centralized apparatus supporting his career. On the other hand, none of this matches the insecurity of his students. These young people frequently equate the values of their faculty with social repression, and yet they are appalled by whatever murky fate awaits them outside the academic rat race. The legions of students flocking into art from science departments expect a release into personal forms of communication and human exchange, unaware that their amateurish numbers will reduce the attention they deserve and the sympathy they might receive from faculty who are old-school enough still to think in terms of high art. Schools remain ill-equipped to house and train a generation of the estranged.

Amidst all this confusion, the museums have evolved

into a deepening quandary. As the amount of purchasable older art declines, or becomes exorbitant for limited acquisition funds, the museums are forced to turn to the open, high-risk area of art in progress as their prime area of responsibility. Some elderly institutions, up to their gills in old masterpieces, refrain from such an unseemly rush into the relevant. (The Philadelphia Museum is an example—while the Metropolitan and the Los Angeles County Museum of Art become ever more internally conflicted in their engagement with new or recent work.) But the general sense of what is happening in museums today obliges us to think of them as the inevitable depots or shipping points for overscaled and undomesticated modern art. The museums, after all, have been enjoying a period of expansion, many of their curators have become competitive, and collector support is still huge. All the more reason, then, to imagine a museological easing of the cultural intestines.

Like the universities, beleaguered by students, the museums, however, are being required to answer to their internal constituencies—the vocal artists—in unexpected ways. At no time has there been a greater range of temporary museum shows devoted to living artists of every conceivable idiom, and at no time has there been greater dissatisfaction among artists about museum exhibition (and purchase) policy.

Partly this is the result of a well-known social mechanism. As previous barriers are lowered, the "barred" grow more demanding. Piecemeal accommodation destabilizes the relationship between the guardians of the gates and those who feel newly franchised to enter. The game suddenly seems playable with different rules. And if that much is granted, then the new rules might as well have to do with any minority's idea of social justice to itself as with esthetic criteria. When an institution like the *late* Washington Gallery of Modern Art devoted itself to sponsoring community and local black artists, it pioneered with uncoerced grace what its fellows are going to be doing awkwardly, and under fire. For if curators are competing incessantly for funds to run their departments, none of them will look eagerly

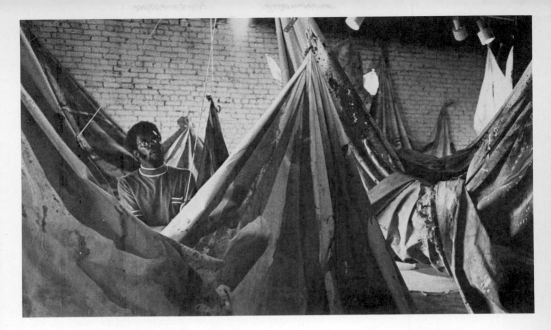

upon the sacrifices to their budget represented by a show
pressured out of the museum by a lobbying group. And
besides the economic injury, there is the psychic insult
of being forced to do something one is very unwilling
to do.

The reason for such unwillingness (if we discount
apathy as simply begging the question) is the insistence
on the part of their personnel that museums do not serve,
nor were ever intended to serve, artists on the basis of
equal representation. No, for some curious reason, they
adhere stubbornly to what they think are their own
exclusive justifications for displaying art, their own
determinants of artistic worth. To be confronted by
such alien demands as that certain percentages of artists
be admitted because of their sex or ethnic background
is to have one's standards as a professional mocked.
Outright accession to such demands may even make a
shambles of the museum's presumed reputation for
"quality" control. And of course the autonomy of the
institution is also threatened—an autonomy which, the
more tenuous it grows, the more glorified it becomes.
These places, the art museums, do strive to preserve an
image of purity when they are asked to do something
inconvenient. This remark is not prompted by sarcasm.
Very real, very large-scale business support looks to

*Sam Gilliam arranging one
of his suspended paintings
in his Washington, D.C.,
studio in the Johnson
Avenue workshop, which is
operated on a grant from
the Corcoran Gallery of
Art, an institution that
has "devoted itself to
sponsoring community and
local black artists . . ."*

rescue the museums from their financial dilemmas, and the staff would prefer that such support not be piqued or made cautious at this delicate moment.

To pursue the matter further is to be overcome by certain paradoxes. It is perfectly true that the camarillas of the museums have followed the lead of patriarchal society in denying women the notice which their accomplishment should have won for itself. How obvious, too, that many museum criteria for choosing shows or buying works are, in effect, more arbitrary and certainly more routinized than the ideas of insurgent groups. But the artists themselves show extreme ambivalence in their attitudes toward museums. They want, on the one hand, to have greater consideration in museum governance, and on the other, to demonstrate contempt for the bureaucratized headquarters of a defunct establishment.

A blending of these contradictory motives has nevertheless taken place under the pressure of the anti-war, anti-imperialist militance that pervades the youth of the country. With some of its more intransigent Young Turk favorites, the New York museum finds itself in a masochistic relationship: staff commitment constantly being tested by outrageous installations, acts of temperament and provocation, ultimatums, sudden withdrawals. The museum that desires to be judged avant-garde pays the price of its pretension by having to bear these frequent disturbances and crises. Conversely, the same museum is made to look callously rejective when it does not extend itself to the entreaties of Puerto Ricans or blacks whose clamor for reform would eliminate many special privileges even as it strives to clear room for the most perfectly orthodox careers. Viewed in this light, the various "advanced" and "ethnic" phalanxes of artistic sensibility on the scene are proving an equal encumbrance to the museum operation, and providing comparable threats to museum identity. Occasionally, a wily director like Thomas Hoving of the Met, tripping the light pragmatic, offers fake concessions to both opponents in a Baroque effort to coast clear. Yet, in general, the museums are in a bind to which their recent internal development contributes as much as any art-political controversy.

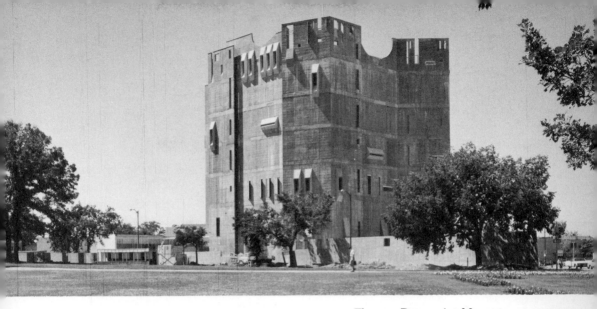

The new Denver Art Museum gives an exemplary illustration of what the author calls "the feudal iconography of the new museums."

Hints of their embattled feelings about themselves are invoked very readily in the architecture of many new museums. A generation or two ago, the typical art institute structure was a serene Greco-Roman temple—for example, the National Gallery or the California Palace of the Legion of Honor, etc. Usually there were possibilities of setting off the temple from the urban hubbub by elevating it on a hill and/or situating it in a park. The authority of its traditional forms would thereby be enhanced by its calming environment. Today such isolation is almost physically impossible to achieve. To compensate, the new museum tends to greet its public in the overly dramatic guise of a bastion, citadel or keep. The Berkeley Art Museum, and the one in Denver, Pasadena's and the Whitney: these are concrete brutes, Cyclopean, or crenellated. They rate extremely low in hospitable appearance, but impress by their fulsome security. Nor is it merely a question of architectural fashion that has shaped these donjons of visual culture, with their eccentric inner spaces. Banks, libraries, colleges and orchestral halls are not brought forth so consistently in this style. The trustee mentality that patronizes such architecture is defensive, very definitely interested in power and dominance, and not overly

155

solicitous of the public. The Renaissance palace accorded very well with the munificent self-image of a J. P. Morgan. The classical pavilions were likely to be the inspiration of municipal or federal will to grandeur. The feudal iconography of the new museums, for their part, is expressive of the corporate network which defines the American economy today.

Gone are the days when the art museums could rely solely on individual philanthropy, or the conceited largess of the industrial barons. Inflation has taken such a toll of the operating expenses of museums that exhibitions would soon, in most cases, have been foreclosed had it not been for a kind of increased grass-roots financing by very large firms like Xerox or American Motors. Already in part underwritten by trustees who are members of many boards, the museum now has to come out in the open as the fief of the corporation.

When business patronized American art in the past, it dealt with single artists who were, themselves, or through their agents, free to accept or reject the commission. But museums are not free-lancers; they have few economic options with which to avoid massive deficits. Of course, hopes are pinned to conceivable high appropriations by Congress for the arts, although so far there has been but a pittance—which, even so, frequently has to be matched by donor corporations. And regardless of its source—government, foundation, municipality or collector—the support is still corporate profit, tax-deductible spin-off, and indirect public subsidy.

In a sense, those famous favorable tax laws which permitted the acquisition and gifting of works of art, works constantly increasing in value, have at long last been converted into a lien on the art world. The more the objects of private collecting reverted to public hands, the more inevitable it became that the economic interests behind that collecting would move to control the public houses of art. Museums are, or will soon be treated like, entities in a conglomerate. Moreover, with a different sponsor for each ambitious exhibition, the museum becomes subject to a carrousel of backers, each feeling entitled to have its interests acknowledged.

Much has been learned about the sibling ties of

many culturally benevolent industries with the war machine and American economic imperialism. Such data is of interest in revealing not only the lack of coincidence between culture and awareness, but the active complicity of the patron class in the repression of people. (Lately, too, galleries and museums in America are being exposed as continual thieves of the art treasures of poor and undeveloped countries.)

But it also has to be admitted that art collecting itself is a would-be monopolistic enterprise, a natural microcosm of the capitalist system, notorious for its tendency to expand on high returns. All those museum directors who insist that the corporate angels exert no influence on their professional practice overlook the fact that investments in our cost-accounting society have to be managed and overseered. Strings are always attached. Mr. Robert Anderson, head of Atlantic-Richfield and chairman of the Business Committee for the Arts, expresses himself as follows: "Corporations should examine the effectiveness of the institutions to which they contribute. There are so many organizations requesting aid that we're going to have to test their value." It would be very enlightening to learn the criteria for that testing. Anderson confines himself to asking, in characteristic fashion, "whether some mergers would not be in order." Given that order, would it be too far-fetched to speculate that the smaller, wobbly, specialized and livelier entrepreneurs (without permanent collections) in the museum field are in danger of being absorbed or forced out?

Faced with outstanding losses incurred by its displays of "advanced" art, the Jewish Museum returns to its neglected Judaica, whose upkeep is also expensive, but more in line with the sentiments of the Jewish Theological Seminary. And everywhere throughout the land there continue those divisions between the claims of developing the older holdings and a consuming involvement with the modern, between older and younger fortunes, between laymen trustees and professional staff members. These thorny problems, structural and personal, have led to many casualties.

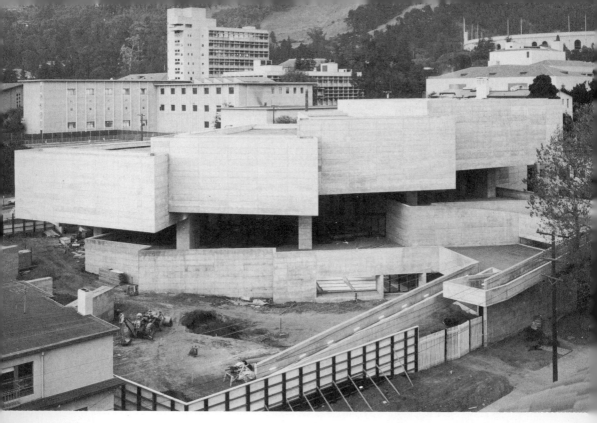

The University Art Museum, University of California, Berkeley. This is one of the newer-style museums that "rate extremely low in hospitable appearance, but impress by their fulsome security."

Such are the tensions that a new breed of director is being imported to assuage them. The present incumbent at the Museum of Modern Art is a tactful administrator with experience in government programs, fund-raising and foundation granting. And the recently appointed director of the Brooklyn Museum seems exemplary in this respect: "National Director of the Canadian Conference of the Arts; President of Janus Museum Consultants, Ltd.; a Director of Cultural Resources Development Corporation . . ." These associations read like a recipe for success in the new art-and-business combine.

In a sense, though, this combine is an arrangement that will hardly solve—in fact, it will even abet—the deepening predicament of the museums. Like so much that afflicts the society, museums are victimized by the phenomenon of growth for its own sake—growth mindless, inhuman, unplanned, existing, consuming, because there is apparently no direction American affairs can take except "more." "The Board of Trustees of the Museum of Fine Arts, Houston, announces a $15 million campaign for new endowment and capital gifts: its paramount objectives are funds to complete the Mies van der Rohe wing of the Museum, and the raising of an acquisitions endowment which will assure the Museum a competitive position in the world art market.'' The language of this museum press release could just as well be that of a stock report. But more significant than that is the lack of any explanation as to why Houston needs the new wing, why the idea of a building comes before that of a collection, and why ''a competitive position in the world art market'' is assumed to be identical with the obligations, services and output of a museum. But this is a standard program, exceptional only in its size. There have been more art museums, far more public square feet of wall and floor devoted to painting and sculpture, erected in the state of California alone than in all of Western Europe in the last twenty years. How are these spaces to be productively filled, even temporarily, if building funds have eaten up those allowed for acquisition? And meanwhile insurance, shipping and conservation are becoming so costly that lending or traveling shows are on their way out. We can only conclude that a corporate obsession has usurped any practical means or restraint in providing a public amenity.

Regardless of whether there are any or enough artists worth being shown, regardless of a community's consciousness of or interest in art, regardless of a people's social priorities, museum buildings sprout up to adorn the pride of the colorless ruling classes. In that sense, they are no different from the moon shots, although requiring far less national expenditure. One might, at least, imagine a redistribution of classic resources from the older, well-endowed museums to the halls of their younger brethren. This would seem rational, since roughly ninety percent of the major museums' permanent collections is never seen. In these precincts, however, the flow of energies and prizes is always co-opted from the smaller to the larger galleries. And the congestion that results from this movement to a few centers buries all over again the chances of reasonable exposure or even retrieval of many treasures. The situation of extreme scarcity and overabundance of art is very reminiscent of a country that is simultaneously enduring an inflation and a recession.

It would seem that a society like ours, committed to its luxuries and indulgences far more than to its necessities, would be one especially sympathetic to art. But we are not Rococo France, nor even the liberal, innocent bourgeois culture that discovered in Abstract Expressionism an abrasive movement of genius in its midst, and then came to honor it. Museums of contemporary art had their meaning then. Much good work can perhaps still be expected from them—retrospectives, mostly. But it is unlikely that such places can long mount shows that reveal important psychic and social tensions in our environment. Those artists who cannot tolerate such tensions will be dropping out of the professional dialogue that makes up art history. The rest will have to take their chances with the glut.

*The Pasadena Art Museum.
"There have been more
art museums, far more public
square feet of wall and
floor devoted to painting
and sculpture, erected
in the state of California
alone, than in all
of Western Europe
in the last twenty years."*

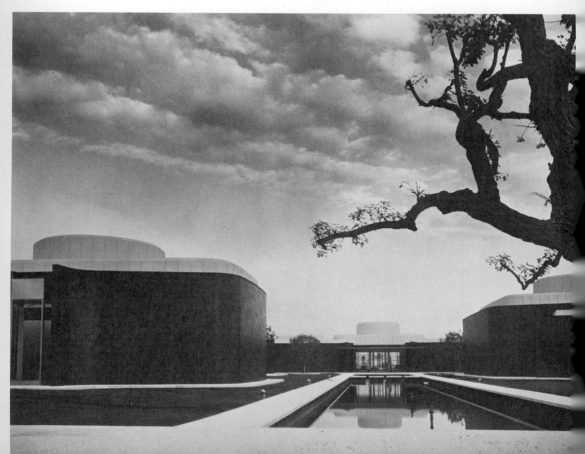

Epilogue: The Dead-Letter Office
HUGH KENNER

"The history of twentieth-century art may someday
appear to have been simply a death struggle with the
museum. In that struggle, art being unkillable,
the museum was foredoomed. Now, the temples
of art history having themselves been relegated to
history (we may speak of the Museum Age, and
contemplate a Museum of Museums), we may expect
art to find more interesting things to do."

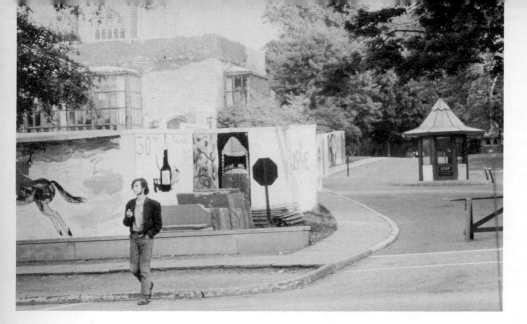

Fences around a construction site on the Princeton University campus were "illuminated" by students; photo Ron Schwerin. "Let the skeleton of a new hive of plaster cubicles commence to be assembled . . . with round it for safety's sake a plyboard fence, and overnight young Giottos modify the assault of that fence with multicolor graffiti."

The State of California, through the Buildings and Grounds Committee of its Multiversity, has supplied me with an office in which to meditate, on the explicit understanding that I affix nothing to the walls. It is a totally puritan interior, a plaster cube. I may inflict no holes, insert no fasteners. The penalties would include, presumably, Visitations and Bills for Damages. A man with a passkey comes in every night to empty the wastebasket, and presumably it is he who checks the walls. The State's postulate is clear: my usefulness to the brightest 10 percent of its adolescents will not be enhanced by rectangular arrangements of form and color.

Which is odd, since the campus does maintain a museum. Or not so odd, since the museum (1) is over by the Art Department, and (2) is a Visual Aid, i.e., an accessory to knowledge otherwise formulated. Understanding, you see, is verbal, discursive (how else could they set examinations?).

Or so they think, but the young don't think so. Let the skeleton of a new hive of plaster cubicles commence to be assembled, to the greater glory of discursive understanding, with round it for safety's sake a plyboard fence, and overnight young Giottos modify the assault of that fence with multicolor graffiti: splashes, circles, Blakean injunctions, intricate polychrome-Tenniel cartooned allegories, the illegible ABCs of psychedelia, clouds and birds of iconic aspiration, fragments of Shelleyan hymns to ecology, the works. You walk past it for months till the building gets up and the fence at last comes down: a transient living *musée sans murs* composed wholly of murals. That's what makes the young feel creative, a piece of environment, a silly piece (plywood slabs); it wants transforming.

So there you have it, the familiar paradigm: no art where you use your mind; dead art where the sign says ART; *tachisme* (and a little better) where nothing is supposed to be and nothing will be for long. I rehearse these details because their environment is officially and institutionally educational. Museums have traditionally been educational, so if the museum-atom is splitting it's on campus that we may find a vector diagram.

Museums have traditionally been educational. What else? In being that they have virtually defined Art. Art is what you can find in a museum. It becomes Art when it is brought there (think of Duchamp's bicycle wheel). Outside where it was made it was an altarpiece, or a bauble for the Medici summer cottage. Once inside the museum it's divorced from context, from any context save a hushed didactic strenuousness. It becomes good for one. For whom? For anyone. Tourists. School-children. Religiose barbarians. Writers of guides. Itinerant professors. Folk in quest of a cool place at lunch hour (but no paper bags beyond the front steps!). Dingily, quietly, the artifacts of an inconceivable past soothe or admonish the comers; a visit to the catacombs is not more salutary, nor (in certain moods) would a trip to the morgue be more macabre. Jeremy Bentham thought it a pity to shovel underground the corpses of great men, and then hire sculptors to make imperfect likenesses. Better, he thought, to set up, suitably stuffed, the very bodies. He was not being sardonic; he was saving work and serving truth. That is not a memorial to the Duke of Wellington; no, that *was* the Duke of Wellington. The one "Auto-Ikon" Bentham achieved was his own. At the University of London they display him, seated in a cabinet, during registration week. But supposing we had Botticelli under

The museum, so considered, has a literary equivalent, the annotated edition, being the repository of poems no longer responded to as formerly, and so turned into teaching machines. At what may be called a dateline in twentieth-century cultural history, in 1922, T. S. Eliot published *The Waste Land* with notes and numbered lines, so creating an instant museum-piece. "The Burial of the Dead," the first section was headed, and sure enough, relics of the mighty dead may be discerned embedded in its mellifluity: Chaucer's April, the Bible's desert and its "Son of Man," Shakespeare's pearled eyes, Dante's weary circling throng, a thrill of Webster's, more; and as for you, ". . . you know only / A heap of broken images . . ." The lines carry numbers, like the lines of official poetry, long dead, and the allusions are itemized, and the "poetry," too, verges on museum-poetry: authorized sonorities, validated *frisson*. At the center of the poem is the myth of the Quester, who enters a ruined temple and notes a miscellany of artifacts. In the myth Eliot took from Jessie Weston's *From Ritual to Romance*, the Quester asks what these forgotten things in fact are, a deed as subversive of quiet as the kind of question Eliot had been asking in the pages of *The Egoist:* "Who, for instance, has a first-hand opinion of Shakespeare?" To ask that is to pluck Shakespeare out of literary history, where his bland stare answers the glazed stares of the docile. When the Quester in the Chapel Perilous asks such questions, then the heavens open, but despite much rumble of thunder Eliot leaves it ambiguous whether or not, in his poem, the question gets properly asked. "Shall I at least set my lands in order?" asks a voice like a desperate curator's on the last page; he proceeds to order exhibits in literary history, from the *Pervigilium Veneris* to *El Desdichado*.

Like its exact contemporary *Ulysses, The Waste Land* seems artfully confected to signify the end of culture. If we look at Eliot's prose of the years just before, we discover many testimonials to his sense that Culture has become synonymous with a Museum Civilization, the dead didactic array. The central metaphor in "Tradition and the Individual Talent'' is the acquisition of today's work by a museum, as though it could have no other destination. Eliot used the word ''monuments'' in an elusively ironical paragraph which notes that ''The existing monuments form an ideal order among themselves.'' And this order is vulnerable, being ''modified by the introduction of the new (the really new) work of art among them.''

''The existing order is complete before the new work arrives; for order to persist after the subvention of novelty, the *whole* existing order must be, if ever so slightly, altered; and so the relations, proportions, values of each work of art toward the whole are readjusted; and this is conformity between the old and the new.'' Behind the impenetrable tone of that final clause we may discern a sardonic recognition of the way the old at first simply *makes room,* but later finds it is tacitly being revalued. Thus Manet's *Le Déjeuner sur l'Herbe* alters our sense of the Giorgione in the Louvre from which its salient motifs are paraphrased. We might not otherwise have reflected that naked women stood about Giorgione's studio, to help him paraphrase the ''classic'' conventions of the allegorical Nude. That *Le Déjeuner,* a scandal for the Second Empire, eventually found its way into the very Louvre where Manet saw the Giorgione, is a sequel almost unbelievably neat. It wasn't carried there damp from the studio; still wilder novelties had to moderate its aggressiveness somewhat, so it could slip in as a bit of Art History.

In a different way from the way previous painters had been conscious of their arrayed predecessors, Manet was conscious that in his time one painted in the shadow of the Louvre. He could not have pretended otherwise. And seizing the initiative, he painted a picture that protests against that fact. Scrub, he implies, the tone of time from the colors; replace Venetian dandies in the costume of their day by Parisian dandies in the costume of our day; remove that look of ''classical'' abstractedness from the nude lady's face—let her self-possessed eyes confront the bourgeois viewer, as though to ask what else he expects if he strays into bohemia—

then pretend, if you can, that "cultural" values are enhanced by Sunday afternoon communion with such an artifact. And the Louvre claimed him after all, for History can subdue anything. It has subdued *The Waste Land* also, and Eliot's poem finds its place today amid the poems with notes and numbered lines in those heaps of broken images, the classroom anthologies it once subverted so vigorously.

Manet and Eliot occupy the two ends of an era we agree has ended, the era called Modernist, which is usually said to have protested with all its vigor against the past. That is not accurate; it protested not against the past, against tradition, but against the didactic uses of the past, and the tradition of the handbook. Insofar as *Le Déjeuner sur l'Herbe* is a satirical painting, it is not Giorgione it satirizes but the Louvre; and *The Waste Land* likewise satirizes Palgrave's *Golden Treasury.* The next step, for painters, since museums always triumphed by buying what they painted after a little wait, was to subvert museums from within, and the history of the various post-Modernisms might be written as a war of the United Artists against the place of cool vaults they had come to think deadly.

Thus about 1917 a curator, roused by the clangor of his doorbell, might shake the cobwebs from his shoulders and swing wide the portals to discover on his marble steps a Duchamp ready-made, the inverted urinal, say, cheekily claiming the right to be admitted. "But you are not sculpture," he splutters, "for you were made in a factory." "Then that Rodin behind you is not sculpture either," responds the urinal, "for it was made in a foundry." "But the Rodin was cunningly and wonderfully designed," rejoins the curator, to whom the urinal: "And do you think my own delicate curves were achieved by accident? They would have enchanted Pythagoras. Observe, moreover, my polished gloss, my pure off-white. A designer stipulated these, craftsmen achieved them; that was not done in a day." "You were made for a low and unmentionable purpose." "Your talk of low and high does not confuse me, and if we are to talk of purposes, the Rodin was made exclusively for the never-mentioned purpose of being sold to someone such as you. And as to the purpose you hint I was made to serve, I no longer mean to serve it, and cheerfully proclaim as much by the fact that I stand before you turned upside down; a procedure, I may add, from which half your collection of sculpture would conceivably profit.'' ''But the Rodin bears the signature of A. Rodin, a sculptor,'' cries the curator, risking his ace. ''As for me,'' says the urinal, ''I bear the signature of R. Mutt.'' ''Who is R. Mutt?'' shrieks the curator. ''Who is A. Rodin?'' rejoins the urinal sweetly. ''Do not say, 'an eminent sculptor,' since your only evidence for that is the agreement of your colleagues and yourself that other things he has signed, no more persuasive than the thing your museum so prides itself on, are pieces of eminent sculpture. And right here, on your doorstep, I propose to sit, until the day comes when you shall have accorded my signer, R. Mutt, as much claim to the title of sculptural eminence as the fabricator of that utterly barbarous likeness of Balzac in which a blasted stump modeled in taffy enshrines the sensibility of a coal-heaver.''

The urinal's point has long since been tacitly conceded, a process a private collector, Walter Arensberg, catalyzed by buying it at once. Soon it had conformed still more closely to the paradigms of classic sculpture by getting lost, even as every piece by Phidias. And even as we guess at Greek sculpture from Roman copies, so at the Sidney Janis Gallery in 1953 one might assess at one remove the sculptural impulse of Mons. Mutt/Duchamp, glimpsed through a replica.

Meanwhile Picasso, leaving behind him a trail of discarded periods, had been performing yet another kind of museum-mimicry. It soon became clear that his Blue Period works, for instance, could be acquired without fear as though they were by a dead artist. No previous painter had done the art-taxonomist's work for him with such thorough effrontery. Soon museums commenced buying easel paintings conceived only decades before as assaults on the museum idea. It could surprise no one that the *Nude Descending a Staircase*, hooted at in 1913 as an explosion in a shingle factory by folk whose perception of heroic paintings did not extend to calling any of them an explosion in a bordello, was received eventually into the Philadelphia Museum of Art.

Impatient with the test of time, Museums of Modern Art arose, hoping to catch creativity on the wing: to capture work done if possible this very morning; whereupon—checkmate!—Jean Tinguely reasoned, and persuaded the New York Museum of Modern Art to credit, that the entire life-cycle of a work of art, from the preparation of the palette, say, to the eventual dropping of decayed paint off the canvas, should be condensed from centuries into a few days, and made to occur in its rightful place, a museum. He fabricated in the museum garden a huge rickety "sculpture" the office of which was to destroy itself, right on the spot, with the firemen in attendance (would there be dynamite? the museum queried), the debris to be carted off by garbagemen. The spectacle was accomplished on St. Patrick's Day, 1960. *The Nation* thought it scented social protest and decried a decline in style (garden parties, not barricades), but the Director of Museum Collections accurately perceived a homage to Art History. "Oh, great brotherhood of Jules Verne, Paul Klee, Sandy Calder, Leonardo da Vinci, Rube Goldberg, Marcel Duchamp, Piranesi, Man Ray, Picabia, Filippo Morghen," he wrote, "are you with it?"

The crowning move of the United Artists was the fabrication, wholesale, of artifacts that can have no conceivable destiny except the museum. The *Nude Descending a Staircase* did time in a private collection, the Elgin Marbles decorated a temple, Holbeins once assuaged the vanity of kings; but imagine a way station, en route to the museum, for a piece consisting of a bar interior with stools on which sit life-sized plaster figures! Such works are instant museum-pieces; there is simply no other place to put them (a living room? Whose?). And an Action Painting bigger than anyone's wall except an institution's, what else can be done with that? They compete in scale with the huge Henry Moores that brood in public courtyards, but being ridiculously perish-

able they can't be set up outdoors. Such works, moreover, have too equivocal a relation with life to be
tolerated for long in the ambiance of any but the most
specialized of existences, such an existence as the one
the gallery-goer assumes when he checks his parcels
just beyond the turnstile. Only the gallery-goer's tran-
sience saves him; such things keep no steady company
but with their own precarious kind, a Pollock, a Segal,
a Giacometti, a Rauschenberg hobnobbing with one another in a world they spin out of one another's proximity:
an art world which is a museum world, an artifice of
eternity where there is no marrying nor giving in
marriage but only the quizzical intercommunion of
artifacts as outrageously unassimilable as dinosaurs.
(Could anyone breed a dinosaur, he would give it *at
once* to a zoo.)

Considered as a technique for destroying museums,
the goings-on in the art world of the sixties had the
frenzied effectiveness of a Laurel and Hardy pie-throw-
ing marathon. The program was radical, perhaps un-

Dennis Oppenheim, Weather Data
Plotted on Bean Field, *Finster-
wolde, Holland, 1969; photo John
Gibson Commissions, Inc.* "Earthworks . . . defy efforts to dig them
up and move them, though a
museum may one day be erected
over the site of one."

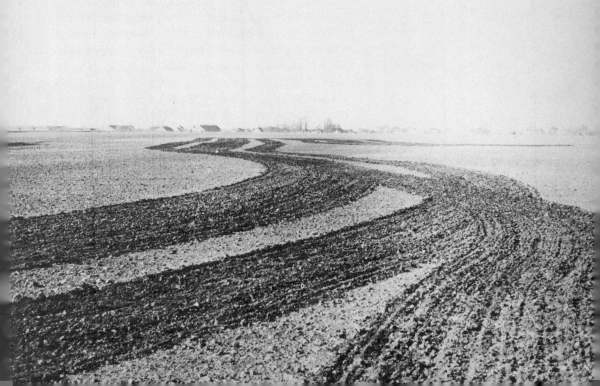

combatable: as fast as new museums could be constructed, to jam them full of huge objects that no one else can house, that would be ruined in the rain, and that no Selection Committee, conscious of its obligations to History, would think of allowing to perish. Rauschenberg's *Goat*, for heaven's sakes, the stuffed one with the tire around its middle, pensive in its junkyard of painted clutter: what else can be done with *that?* The Moderna Museet, Stockholm, saw its obligation. And more, and more. It resembled an effort at jamming the postal service by addressing tons of mail to the Dead-Letter Office.

Then suddenly the strategy shifted. Instead of art that could only go into museums, art began to be turned out that museums couldn't get at. Earthworks, for instance, defy efforts to dig them up and move them, though a museum may one day be erected over the site of one, and a kinetic sculpture of dyes dropped into a stream will resist all efforts to fit it under a roof in however grandiose a maxi-Jacuzzi. Having goaded the museum mind to a frenzy of blind acquisitiveness, the artist's new ploy is to taunt it with the non-acquirable. Very soon curators, teased beyond bearing, will commence going mad. Their office is to institutionalize Art History, and Art History, so far as they can display it, will seem to have stopped short in the late 1960s, having stepped into a new dimension, out of reach. As for the Ideal Order which Eliot confronted, the order modulated when at long intervals it nodded assent to "the really new," but an order still calm, still constituted of "monuments," still capable of housebreaking a *fauve,* that order stopped decades ago. The history of twentieth-century art may someday appear to have been simply a death struggle with the museum. In that struggle, art being unkillable, the museum was foredoomed. Now, the temples of art history having themselves been relegated to history (we may speak of the Museum Age, and contemplate a Museum of Museums), we may expect art to find more interesting things to do.

Perhaps much that is in museums will be silently returned to where it came from, the Elgin Marbles for

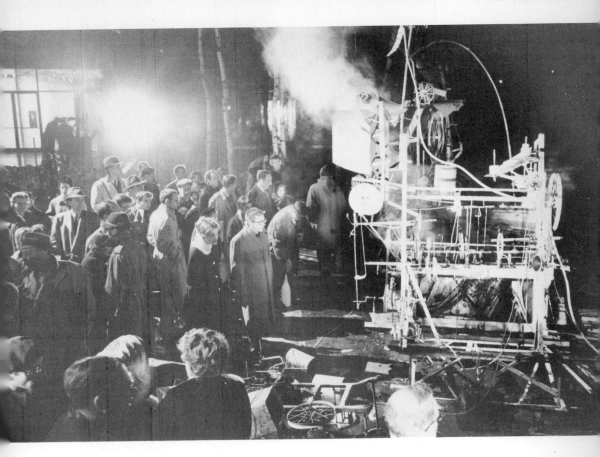

Jean Tinguely, Homage to New
York, *March 17, 1960.*
Museum of Modern Art garden,
New York. Onlookers collecting
souvenirs from smoking heap;
photo, The New York Times.
"He fabricated in the museum
garden a huge rickety
'sculpture' the office of
which was to destroy itself,
right on the spot,
with the firemen in attendance
. . . the debris to be
carted off by garbagemen."

instance back to the Acropolis. Athens is now as accessible as London. A transparent dome would protect them from further erosion; surely some disciple of Fuller's will oblige. And the Rubenses, might they not go back to Flanders, and the Munich and London Botticellis to Florence, and the Mantegnas to the Ducal Palace in Mantua? And finally, gathered into a last Museum, those works that never had any other destination. In some Temple of the End of Art History, a terminal moraine, there the Goat, girdled by its tire, will commune thoughtfully forever with the plaster denizens of the bar, who in turn, their backs forever turned to the giant plastic hamburgers, will avoid staring at, or will stare with unseeing plaster eyes at, the thirty-two-foot Hard Edge, its dogmatism offset by the frozen insouciance of a huge dribble from which a Giacometti stick-man strides motionless forever away. And the University may let me put a nail in my wall when I find a picture I like. The fences, though—the kids will go on painting fences, and contractors will pull them down regardless, the paintings having lasted as long as they needed to. Much that's in Art Museums has lasted much longer than that.

Notes on the Contributors

JOHN E. BOWLT

Studied in England before taking a two-year research appointment at Moscow University, where he made a detailed study of Russian painting. He is presently teaching Russian language, literature, and art at the University of Texas at Austin under the auspices of the Woodrow Wilson Fellowship Foundation. He is the author of many articles on modern Russian art and has just completed a book entitled *Modern Russian Masters* (to be published in 1972).

EDWARD F. FRY

Studied at Princeton, Harvard, and the Sorbonne. He has taught at several major American universities including Princeton and Yale. His involvement with museum work began in 1959; from 1967 to 1971 he was associate curator at the Solomon R. Guggenheim Museum. He is the author of *Cubism* (1966) and *David Smith* (1969).

GRACE GLUECK

Studied at Washington Square College and Columbia University. She has been a Sunday columnist for *The New York Times* since 1964, and is a regular contributor to its Sunday *Magazine* and *Book Review*, *The New Republic*, *American Heritage*, and *Art in America*.

HUGH KENNER

Studied in Canada and at Yale. He has been Professor of English at the University of California at Santa Barbara since 1950, and is the author of numerous articles and books, among them *Wyndham Lewis* (1954), *Dublin's Joyce* (1962), *Samuel Beckett, A Critical Study* (1968), *The Invisible Poet: T. S. Eliot* (1959), and *The Counterfeiters, an Historical Comedy* (1968). His X-ray moving picture of an age, entitled *The Pound Era*, will soon appear in book form.

MAX KOZLOFF
A member of the faculty of the California Institute of the Arts, in Valencia. He is the author of *Jasper Johns* (1968) and *Renderings* (1969).

THOMAS W. LEAVITT
Studied at Middlebury College, and at Boston and Harvard universities. He served as director and assistant director of several major art museums, and as first director of the museum program at the National Endowment for the Arts in Washington, D.C. Presently director of the Andrew Dickson White Museum of Art at Cornell University and Professor of Art History at Cornell, he is the author of numerous exhibition catalogs and articles, and is currently preparing for the opening of a new I. M. Pei design museum at Cornell.

LINDA NOCHLIN
Studied at Vassar College, and at Columbia and New York universities. She has served as Professor of Art History at Vassar and Visiting Professor of Art History at Hunter College. The author of *Realism and Tradition in Art, 1848–1900: Sources and Documents* (1966); *Impressionism and Post–Impressionism, 1874–1904: Sources and Documents* (1966); and *Realism* (1971), she is also a regular contributor to *The Art Bulletin, Art News,* and *Art Forum.*

BRYAN ROBERTSON
Was art critic of *The Spectator* from 1964 to 1970. He is presently director of the museum on the new campus of the State University of New York at Purchase. He was the editor of *Jackson Pollock* (1960).

JOHN SPENCER
Studied at Yale University. He has taught at Yale, the University of Florida, and Oberlin College., He is presently Professor of Art and Director of the Allen Memorial Art Museum at Oberlin College, and was recently appointed to the museum advisory panel of the National Endowment for the Arts.

ERNEST VAN DEN HAAG

Studied at New York University, the universities of Naples and Florence, and the Sorbonne. He is Adjunct Professor of Social Philosophy at NYU, and is a practicing psychoanalyst. His many books include *The Fabric of Society* (1957), *Passion and Constraint* (1962), and *The Jewish Mystique* (1969). He is a contributor to a number of American and European journals.